Student Support
Materials

Edexcel A2 History

Unit 3 D1

From Kaiser to Führer: Germany, 1900–45

Series editor: Angela Leonard

Authors: Alan White and Adam Bloomfield

William Collins' dream of knowledge for all began with the publication of his first book in 1819. A self-educated mill worker, he not only enriched millions of lives, but also founded a flourishing publishing house. Today, staying true to this spirit, Collins books are packed with inspiration, innovation and practical expertise. They place you at the centre of a world of possibility and give you exactly what you need to explore it.

Collins. Freedom to teach

Published by Collins
An imprint of HarperCollins*Publishers*
77 – 85 Fulham Palace Road
Hammersmith
London
W6 8JB

Browse the complete Collins catalogue at
www.collinseducation.com

© HarperCollins*Publishers* Limited 2012

10 9 8 7 6 5 4 3 2 1

ISBN-13 978 0 00 745743 4

Alan White and Adam Bloomfield assert their moral rights to be identified as the authors of this work

British Library Cataloguing in Publication Data
A Catalogue record for this publication is available from the British Library

Commissioned by Andrew Campbell
Project managed by Alexandra Riley and Shirley Wakley
Production by Simon Moore

Designed by Jouve
Edited by Joan Miller
Proofread by Joan Miller and Grace Glendinning
Indexed by Michael Forder
Illustrations by Ann Paganuzzi
Picture and text research by Grace Glendinning and Caroline Green
Cover picture research by Caroline Green
Cover design by Angela English
With special thanks to: Kimberley Atkins for devising the concept

Printed and bound by Printing Express Limited, Hong Kong

COVER: Adolf Hitler (1889–1945) addresses soldiers with his back facing the camera at a Nazi rally in Dortmund, Germany. Supplied by Mary Evans/Rue des Archives/Tallandier.

Acknowledgements
The publishers gratefully acknowledge the permission granted to reproduce the copyright material in this book. While every effort has been made to trace and contact copyright holders, where this has not been possible the publishers will be pleased to make the necessary arrangements at the first opportunity.

p 6 from Ralf Roth, Between *Reform and Revolution: German Socialism and Communism*, *1840–1990*, edited by David E.
Barclay & Eric D. Weitz © David E. Barclay and Eric D. Weitz. Reproduced by permission of Berghahn Books Inc; p 15 from Volker Berghahn, *Imperial Germany 1871–1918* © 2005 Volker R. Berghahn. Reproduced by permission of Berghahn Books Inc; p 21 from Paul Kennedy, *The Rise and Fall of the Great Powers*, published 1988 by Random House Inc.; p 23 from Norman Stone, *World War One: A Short History*, published 2007 by Allen Lane. By permission of Penguin.; p 25t from James Joll, *The Origins of the First World War*, published by Pearson Education © The Estate of Professor James Joll and Gordon Martel 2007; p 25c from A.J.P. Taylor, *The Course of German History*, published 1961 by Methuen & Co Ltd., subsequent editions by Routledge; p 27 from David Thomson, *Europe since Napoleon*, published by A.A. Knopf, 1966; p 29 from Immanuel Geiss, 'Origins of the First World War' in H.W. Koch (editor), *The Origins of the First Word War*, published 1972 by MacMillan; p 33, 109 & 130b from Niall Ferguson, *The Pity of War*, published by Allen Lane, Copyright © 1999 Niall Ferguson. Reprinted by permission of Basic Books, a member of the Perseus Books Group and by permission of Penguin; p 37 from M.S. Seligmann and R.R. Mclean, *Germany from Reich to Republic*, 1871–1918, 2000, published by MACMILLAN PRESS LTD. Reproduced with permission of Palgrave Macmillan; p 68 from Adam LeBor and Roger Boyes, *Seduced by Hitler*, published 2000 by Sourcebooks; p 74 & 137b from Robert Gellately, *Backing Hitler: Consent and Coercion in Nazi Germany*, published 2001. By Permission of Oxford University Press; pp 76–77 & 137t from Richard Evans, *The Third Reich in Power*, published 2005 by Allen Lane. By permission of Penguin; p 80 Excerpt from Hitler's *Weltanschauung* by Eberhard Jäckel, trans. Herbert Arnold © 1972 by Wesleyan University. Reprinted by permission of Wesleyan University Press; p 82 from Joseph Bendersky, *A History of Nazi Germany*, published in 1956 by Rowman & Littlefield Publishing Group and reproduced with permission; p 83 from Ian Kershaw, *Hitler, the Germans and the Final Solution*, published 2008 by Yale University Press © 2008 by Ian Kershaw; p 84 from Martin Broszat, *The Hitler State*, published in 1981 by Longman; pp 84–85 from Lucy S. Dawidowicz, *The War against the Jews 1933–45*, published in 1975 by Holt, Rinehart and Winston; p 86 from Lizzie Collingham, *The Taste of War: World War Two and the Battle for Food*, published in 2011 by Allen Lane. By permission of Penguin and Aitken Alexander Associates; p 107 & 130t from David Blackbourn, *History of Germany 1780–1918*, published in 1997 by Fontana Press and in 2002 by Blackwell Publishing; p 108 & 130c from THE ORIGINS OF THE FIRST WORLD WAR by L.F.C. Turner. Copyright © 1970 by L.F.C. Turner, published by W. W. Norton & Company, Inc; p 137c from Eric Johnson, *Nazi terror: the Gestapo, Jews, and ordinary Germans*, published in 1999 by Perseus Books in US and Hodder & Stoughton in the UK.

The publisher would like to thank the following for permission to reproduce pictures in these pages (t = top, b = bottom, c = centre, l = left, r = right):

COVER Mary Evans/Rue des Archives/Tallandier; p 13 World History Archive/Alamy; p 27 Karikatur-album, C. E. Jensen, 1906. Signed "Bernard Partridge"/WikiMedia Commons; p 60 WikiMedia Commons.

Contents

Economic expansion: the growth of industry c1900–14

Industrialisation

In the late 19th century and early 20th century, Imperial Germany
underwent an economic and social transformation. The growth of industry
was accompanied by urbanisation, improvements in communications and
the emergence of new social classes. Societies experiencing changes of this
kind are said by social scientists to be undergoing modernisation. Pre-1914
Imperial Germany was a society in the throes of modernisation. The years
between 1900 and 1914 were ones of especially rapid change.

Features of Germany's economic development, 1900–14

1900–14 Germany experienced a period of rapid and almost uninterrupted
economic growth. Industrial output rose dramatically. In just over a
decade, coal and iron production doubled and steel production tripled. It
added up to 'a whirlwind boom period' (Hans-Ulrich Wehler, *The German
Empire, 1871–1918*, 1985).

In the years before 1914, high-technology industries emerged as the
leading sectors in the German economy. In the 1870s and 1880s Germany
was viewed elsewhere as a manufacturer of low-priced goods produced by
cheap labour. By 1914 its reputation was very different: it had established a
preeminent position in Europe in the key industries of the 'Second
Industrial Revolution' – steel, chemicals, electrical engineering and
automobile engineering.

Germany's high-technology industries benefited from close links with its
renowned scientific community. In the 1900s German scientists led the
world. Between 1901 – the year Nobel Prizes were first awarded – and 1914,
Germans won a third of all the science prizes. An example of German
scientific discovery that had huge commercial potential was the Haber
process for 'fixing' nitrogen (1909), which allowed artificial fertilisers to be
produced on an industrial scale.

The early 20th-century German economy exhibited a high degree of industrial
concentration – that is, it was dominated by a small number of very large firms.
The largest German companies were industrial giants capable of sweeping all
before them on world markets. The tycoons who headed these concerns,
almost all of them political conservatives, had considerable political clout. The
Ruhr steel dynasties, the Krupps and the Thyssens are cases in point.

Some major early 20th-century German companies

Steel	Chemical	Electrical	Automobiles
Krupps	BASF	Siemens	Benz
Thyssen	Bayer	Bosch	Daimler
	Hoechst	AEG	
	Agfa		

Rapid economic growth 1900–14 meant full employment and a favourable
bargaining position for trades unions. Between 1900 and 1914 trades union
membership rose from 0.8 million to 2.4 million. The biggest trades unions
(the so-called 'Free Trades Unions') were linked to the Social Democratic
Party (SPD): conservative industrial tycoons viewed their growth with alarm.

Centres of industry

The impact of industrial growth in Germany was uneven. Some regions of the country remained largely rural and agricultural: farmers, peasants and agricultural labourers accounted for one-third of Germany's labour force in 1914. The main centres of industry were the Ruhr, Berlin, Saxony and Silesia.

Germany and its centres of industry

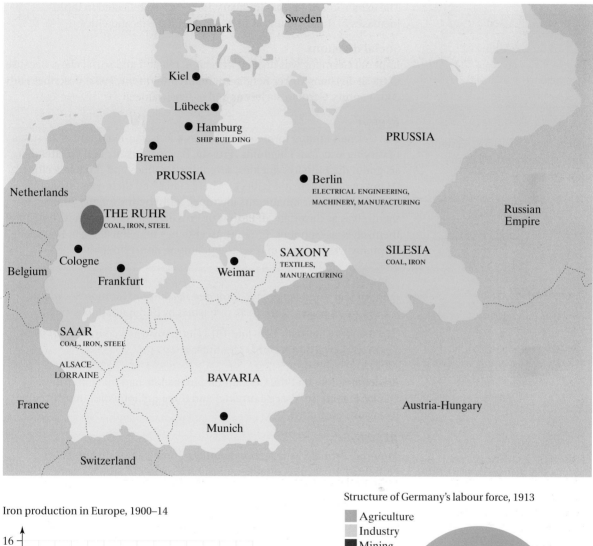

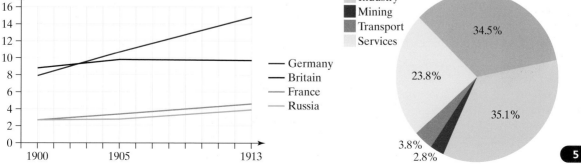

Iron production in Europe, 1900–14

Germany
Britain
France
Russia

Structure of Germany's labour force, 1913

Agriculture
Industry
Mining
Transport
Services

34.5%
23.8%
35.1%
3.8%
2.8%

Essential notes

The populations (in millions) of some major industrial cities, 1900–14, are listed in the table.

	1900	1910
Berlin	1.89	2.17
Hamburg	0.71	0.93
Düsseldorf	0.21	0.36
Essen	0.12	0.30
Duisburg	0.93	0.23

(Note that Düsseldorf, Essen and Duisburg are all in the Ruhr.)

Religious affiliation in Germany, 1910

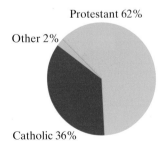

Protestant 62%

Other 2%

Catholic 36%

Imperial Germany: social divisions

Population growth

Germany before 1914 was in the throes of demographic as well as economic change. In the years 1871–1914 Germany's population increased by 40 per cent. Population growth contributed to people's sense of living in a society in flux.

The expansion of German industry 1900–14 was reflected in rapid increases in the populations of its industrial towns and cities.

Social divisions

Imperial Germany was divided by region, religion and social class. Because of these divisions Volker Berghahn (*Modern Germany*, 1982) describes early 20th-century German society as 'full of tension'.

Region

The German Empire formed in 1871 was a Prussian-led union of 25 states of varying size: four kingdoms (Prussia, Bavaria, Saxony and Württemberg), six grand duchies, five duchies, seven principalities and three free cities (Hamburg, Bremen and Lübeck). These states had their own distinctive histories and their inhabitants identified with them strongly, thinking of themselves as Bavarians or Saxons or Prussians as much as they thought of themselves as Germans. Prussia's ascendancy in political life in Imperial Germany was a source of resentment among non-Prussians.

> **Source 1**
> (From Ralf Roth, *Between Reform and Revolution: German Socialism and Communism, 1840–1990*, published by Berghahn Books 1998)
>
> In the years between 1848 and 1914 Germany was a country marked by powerful local and regional identities.

Remember, too, that the German Empire had its national minorities: Danes, French (in Alsace-Lorraine) and three million Poles (mostly living in eastern Germany).

Religion

Imperial Germany was preponderantly a Protestant state but it also contained a sizeable Catholic minority. Germany's Catholics were concentrated in three main areas: Bavaria, the Rhineland and Silesia.

In the early years of the German Empire the Prussian ruling class viewed German Catholics with suspicion, believing that they took their orders from the Vatican. These suspicions gave rise to the so-called *Kulturkampf* of the 1870s – a campaign by the government to undermine the influence of the Catholic Church in Germany. In response, Catholics formed their own political party, the Centre Party or *Zentrum*. The *Kulturkampf* was abandoned in the late 1870s and religious tensions eased. However, anti-Catholic prejudice did not entirely disappear.

Social class

The most important way in which German society was divided was by social class. Early 20th-century Germany was a strongly hierarchical society in which social mobility – movement between social classes – was limited.

At the top of the social pyramid were the conservative elites: at the bottom were the industrial working class and agricultural labourers. Between them was a large and diversified middle class.

Germany's social structure, 1914

Conservative elites
- The core elite was the Prussian aristocracy, the *Junkers*, owners of wheat and rye-producing estates in eastern Germany.
- Closely connected with the *Junkers* were the officer corps of the German army and major industrialists, especially the coal and steel 'barons' of the Ruhr.

Middle classes
The main sub-groups within the middle classes were:
- prosperous merchants, industrialists and businessmen
- the educated and professional middle class – lawyers, doctors, teachers
- self-employed small businessmen, including shopkeepers (the *Mittelstand*)
- salaried middle-managers and office workers.

Working classes and agricultural labourers
- The working class was the largest group in German society: around 40% of all Germans in 1914 were workers.
- German workers were poorly integrated into German society, mostly living apart in working class ghettoes.
- In response to its isolation, the German working class developed its own tight-knit sub-culture. At the heart of it lay the Social Democratic Party, which made cultural and educational provision for its supporters as well as representing them politically.

Four social-political camps

Politics in Imperial Germany did not revolve solely around class and class conflict. Regionalism and especially religion cut across class divisions and were complicating factors. Some German historians have therefore argued that early 20th-century German society is best understood as consisting of four social-political 'camps': the conservative camp (populated by the conservative elites), the middle-class camp, the Catholic camp and the working-class camp.

Key to an understanding of early 20th-century German politics is an awareness of the deeply hostile attitude of the conservative camp to the working-class camp. Conservatives feared and hated the Social Democratic Party, believing that its hostility to capitalism and its commitment to equality represented a threat to their own wealth and power. The rapid growth of the SPD in the years before 1914 (see page 11) increased these fears.

Essential notes

This Constitution came into operation when the German Empire was founded and remained in force, unamended, in 1900. It was replaced by the Weimar Constitution in 1919.

Imperial Germany: government and constitution

The 1871 Constitution

The 1871 Constitution established a federal system of government in unified Germany. In a federation, political authority is shared between a central (or federal) government and a number of state (or regional) governments.

Constitution of the German Empire, 1871

The diagram shows the key institutions of the federal and state governments, and the division of responsibilities between the federal government and the states

The Emperor (Kaiser)
- Appointed and dismissed (federal) government ministers
- Commander in chief of the armed forces
- Controlled foreign policy, including declaring war and making treaties
- Could dissolve the Reichstag and force a general election

Imperial Chancellor
- Appointed by the Emperor
- Was the Emperor's chief minister
- Other government ministers were accountable to the Imperial Chancellor

State goverments
- The 25 individual states were responsible for policing, education and social welfare and could raise their own taxes
- With the exception of the 'free cities' of Hamburg, Lübeck and Bremen, state governments were headed by the hereditary kings, princes, grand dukes and dukes who had ruled before 1871

Federal Council
- An assembly of representatives of the 25 states
- State delegations varied in number depending on the size of the state
- The Federal Council's consent was required for any new law

The Reichstag
- The national parliament
- Shared law-making power with Federal Council: had the right to discuss, amend, pass or reject government proposals for new laws
- Could not initiate legislation
- Government ministers were not accountable to the Reichstag

State parliaments
Most states had their own elected law-making assembly (or *Landtag*)

State electorates
- Each state decided its own electoral arrangements
- In Prussia there was a three-tier franchise which gave a disproportionate amount of political influence to the wealthy

Federal electorate
All German men over the age of 25 had the right to vote in Reichstag elections

The role of Prussia

Prussia accounted for around two-thirds of both the land area and population of the German Empire. It was also the dominant influence in the politics of the Empire:

- Under the 1871 Constitution the King of Prussia was also German Emperor.

- The Minister–President of Prussia was Imperial Chancellor.

- Prussia had 17 of 58 seats on the Federal Council, three more than the 14 needed to block any change to the 1871 Constitution.

- Imperial affairs were largely administered by Prussian civil servants.

- Prussian troops were by far the biggest contingent in the Empire's army.

Was Imperial Germany an autocratic state?

William II often spoke as if he wielded autocratic power. 'The Empire has but one leader and I am he,' he declared in 1891. The constitutional position was not as clear-cut as this claim suggested. The reality was that the Emperor was powerful but not all-powerful:

- The Emperor had no control over matters for which the individual states retained responsibility.

- The Emperor and his ministers could not change the law without the approval of the Federal Council and the Reichstag. This meant, among other things, that the Reichstag had to approve the annual Imperial budget and (every seven years) the military budget. The Reichstag was far from powerless.

The political role of William II

Historians disagree about the precise nature of William II's role in German politics between 1890 and 1918. Some see his reign as a period of 'personal rule'. Others maintain that the political agenda in these years was largely set by Germany's conservative elites.

A number of points can be made in support of the idea of 'personal rule':

- William II's intention at the start of his reign was to be a 'hands-on' ruler in a way previous emperors had not been.

- William II's ministers only survived if they retained his support.

- William II intervened decisively in the political process on numerous occasions.

On the other hand:

- Impulsive and erratic, William II was, by temperament, unsuited to govern on a day-to-day basis.

- He had little interest in the details of domestic policy.

- His interest in the business of government faded as time went on.

- He did not have a coherent personal agenda that he imposed on his ministers.

Essential notes

Note that the Prussian three-tier franchise was used in elections to the Prussian state parliament and *not* in Reichstag elections. The three-tier franchise was the basis of *Junker* power in Prussian affairs – it gave them and their allies the ability to choose 85% of members of the state parliament. Abolishing the three-tier system was one of the main political aims of liberals and progressives in Germany before 1914.

Examiners' notes

The Examination Specification states that candidates should have an understanding of the relative powers of the Kaiser, Chancellor and Reichstag. The word 'relative' here is key. One thing to focus on is the extent of the Reichstag's power to influence the composition and policies of the government. Another is the position of the Chancellor in relation to the Emperor: note that although Chancellors did not have any constitutional power to restrain the Emperor they were often, in practice, able to do so.

Imperial Germany: political parties and pressure groups

Political parties

The party system, which took shape in Germany in the 1860s and 1870s, survived broadly intact into the Weimar era. It was a multi-party system. Each of the four social-political camps had its own political party or parties.

The conservative camp

There were two conservative parties in Imperial Germany: the German Conservative Party (DKP) and the Free Conservatives (RFKP). Both were anti-democratic and strongly anti-socialist. Where they differed was in the nature of their support. The German Conservative Party represented the Prussian *Junkers* while the Free Conservatives were the party of non-Prussian landowners and major industrialists.

The middle-class camp

The National Liberals drew their support from the wealthier elements in the middle classes, especially the business community. Notionally a pro-democracy liberal party, the National Liberals had by the 1900s moved to the right, their anti-socialism and support for an expansionist foreign policy giving them common ground with conservatives.

After 1871, the Left Liberals underwent a series of splits and mergers before uniting in 1910, with the formation of the Progressive People's Party. Backed largely by the educated middle class, the Left Liberals wanted more power for the Reichstag and favoured social reform.

The Catholic camp

The Centre Party represented Catholics of all social classes. Supporters of the Centre Party were united in their desire to defend the interests of the Catholic Church but were divided on other issues.

The working-class camp

The Social Democratic Party (*Sozialdemokratische Partei Deutschlands,* or SPD), founded in 1875, represented the fast-growing German working class. Its support was strongest among skilled workers. Nominally, the SPD was a Marxist party. Its Erfurt Programme (1891) committed it to the establishment of socialism by revolutionary means. In practice, committed revolutionaries were in a minority within the SPD. Most SPD activists were 'revisionists' who believed in reform rather than revolution and sought to advance the socialist cause by democratic means.

German political parties, 1900: a summary

Conservative camp		Middle-class camp		Catholic camp	Working-class camp
DKP	RFKP	National Liberals	Left Liberals	Centre Party	SPD

Essential notes

Edward Bernstein (1850–1932), a leading SPD theorist, challenged Marx's claim that revolution was inevitable in capitalist societies. Bernstein argued: the poor got better off under capitalism, not ever poorer as Marx alleged; the downfall of capitalism was not therefore inevitable; socialism could only be established by democratic methods. Orthodox Marxists labelled these ideas 'revisionist'.

Political parties and the *Kaiserreich*

The Emperor's ministers in the 1900s could, for the most part, rely on the support of the conservative parties and the National Liberals. On many issues they were able to win the backing of the Centre Party, especially its right wing. The Left Liberals and the Social Democrats opposed government policy on most but not all issues. The growth of the oppositionist SPD was a matter of deep concern to Germany's conservative elites. In 1912 the SPD became the largest single party in the Reichstag.

Reichstag election results, 1898–1912 (% share of the vote, rounded)

	1898	1903	1907	1912
Conservative parties	16	14	14	12
National Liberals	13	14	14	14
Left Liberals	11	9	11	12
Centre	19	20	19	16
Social Democrats	27	24	29	35
Others	14	19	13	11

Note that support for the other major parties was broadly static in the 1900s.

Pressure groups and the press

Wilhelmine Germany was not a state in which there was rigid censorship or limitations on the ability to express political opinions freely.

There was, in Wilhelmine Germany, a free press that could be strongly critical of the government. Newspapers and magazines opposed to the government included *Vowärts* (Forward), the Social Democratic Party newspaper and the satirical magazine *Simplicissimus*.

Pressure groups also flourished in Wilhelmine Germany. Among the most active and influential were right-wing pressure groups calling for an expansionist foreign policy, increased military and naval spending and the acquisition of colonies:

- the Colonial Society (founded 1887)
- the Pan–German League (founded 1893)
- the Navy League (founded 1898: claimed to have over 300 000 fully paid-up members and 700 000 other supporters).

Examiners' notes

The Examination Specification requires you to be aware of the impact of economic and social changes on politics and political parties between 1900 and 1914. The key points may be summarised as follows:

1. As a result of industrial growth the German working class was rapidly increasing in size.
2. The growth of the working class led to increased support for the SPD. In 1898 2.1 million Germans voted for the SPD; 4.2 million did so in 1912.
3. Germany's conservative elites saw the SPD's socialism as a threat to their wealth and their political power. They were further alarmed by the growth of the SPD-linked trades unions.
4. The conservative elites were preoccupied in the 1900s with keeping the SPD – who they saw as 'enemies of the Reich' – at bay, but this was not easy to do without violating the constitution.
5. The Centre Party was losing some of its support among the Catholic working class to the SPD.

Domestic politics, 1900–14

Domestic politics in Wilhelmine Germany revolved around:

- the relationship within the government between William II and his Chancellors

- the relationship between the government (the Emperor and his ministers) on the one hand and the legislature (the Reichstag) on the other.

William II and his Chancellors, 1900–14

William's first two Chancellors, Caprivi (1890–4) and Hohenlohe (1894–1900), both made enemies of the *Junkers* and paid the price.

Bülow (1900–09) survived longer than his predecessors, mainly because he was a shrewd political operator, handling the Reichstag adroitly and flattering the Emperor shamelessly. His positive achievements as Chancellor, though, were limited. Bülow's relationship with William II eventually broke down over the *Daily Telegraph* affair.

Theobald von Bethmann-Hollweg (1909–17) was a competent, low-key, unadventurous bureaucrat. He was certainly not a commanding figure who dominated the political scene. His one attempt to seize the political initiative – his bid in 1910 to reform the three-tier Prussian electoral system – ended in failure.

The government and the Reichstag

Early 20th-century German Chancellors seeking Reichstag approval for changes in the law faced a difficult task. The political parties most in tune with the government – the Conservatives and the National Liberals – were in a minority in the Reichstag from 1890 onwards. Governments, therefore, had to win support for their proposals from one or more of the parties of the centre and the left. They used a range of methods to do so:

- The simplest tactic available to William II's Chancellors was bargaining. In the early 1900s, for instance, Bülow repealed an anti-Jesuit law, a relic of the *Kulturkampf*, and passed a series of social welfare reforms in return for Centre Party support elsewhere.

- William II's Chancellors employed the tactic of seeking to unite the conservative elites and middle classes around a programme of imperialism and anti-socialism. This was *Sammlungspolitik* – literally, the 'politics of bringing together'. The building of the German navy, for example, was, in part, intended to win the middle classes over to the *Kaiserreich*. *Sammlungspolitik* did not, however, turn the middle-class parties into unqualified supporters of the regime: allegations of military brutality in German south-west Africa (1904–5) and Zabern (1913) saw them siding with its critics.

Essential notes

In 1908 the *Daily Telegraph* published an article quoting indiscreet remarks about British foreign policy that had been made by William II, in conversation with a friend. In Germany a political row broke out in which the Emperor was accused of being an embarrassment to his country. It turned out that William had given an advance copy of the article to Bülow, who had cleared it for publication. Under pressure, Bülow tried to deflect the blame for what had happened back on to the Emperor. William felt betrayed by Bülow and wanted rid of him.

Essential notes

With the Social Democrats more or less political outcasts and the Left Liberals lacking numbers, William II's Chancellors looked mainly to the Centre Party for support. It was keen to prove its loyalty to the Empire and controlled about a quarter of the seats in the Reichstag.

- When in difficulty, Chancellors always had the option of dissolving the Reichstag in the hope those fresh elections would see their critics defeated. This is what Bülow did in the 'Hottentot' election of 1907.

- Conservatives argued that, in the last resort, a government faced with an uncontrollable Reichstag should disband it by force and rule without it – that is, carry out a military coup.

The Zabern incident revealed the true nature of the relationship between the Kaiser, Chancellor and Reichstag. The incident is discussed in detail on the next two pages.

The Zabern incident: a German cartoon showing powerless inhabitants of Alsace terrorised by a larger-than-life Prussian offficer

Essential notes

In the election that followed the dissolution of the Reichstag, Bülow waged an aggressive and successful campaign in defence of the government's record in German south-west Africa. The term 'Hottentot' was used by European colonists to describe the indigenous population of German south-west Africa.

☞ **Continued on the next two pages**

Essential notes

The Emperor's powers, in relation to the army, were defined by Article 63 of the 1871 Constitution: 'The entire land forces of the Empire will form a single army which in war and peace is under the command of the Emperor.'

The Zabern incident, 1913

The incident

In 1913, a 20-year-old German army officer, Lieutenant von Forstner, stationed at Zabern in Alsace, ordered recruits to respond violently if attacked by any of the local civilians, to whom he referred by the derogatory term '*Wackes*'. News of the order somehow found its way into the local press and led to a demonstration that the army robustly suppressed, unlawfully arresting some of the demonstrators. There was then a separate incident in which von Forstner viciously assaulted a Zabern shoemaker who shouted abuse at him in the street.

The army's response

The army stood by its men. Von Forstner was given a reprimand – a mere slap on the wrist – for the original '*Wackes*' incident. He was subsequently court-martialled for assaulting the shoemaker but was acquitted. Also acquitted by a court-martial was the senior officer (Colonel von Reuter) responsible for the unlawful arrests at the Zabern demonstration.

The political fall-out

The Zabern incident led to a wave of protest across Germany. Demonstrations against the army took place in all of the country's main industrial centres. These demonstrations were orchestrated by the Social Democratic Party.

In December 1913 a Reichstag motion censuring Bethmann-Hollweg, the Chancellor, was passed 293–54. The National Liberals, the Left Liberals and the Centre Party joined the Social Democrats in voting for the motion: only the Conservatives voted against it.

Significance of the Zabern incident

Civil–military relations

The Zabern incident demonstrated that the army was accountable only to the Emperor and not to the civilian authorities. If the Emperor sided with the army, as he did in the Zabern affair, it was untouchable. In Imperial Germany the political influence of the army was concealed by the outward appearance of civilian rule: Zabern offered a reminder of how great its influence was.

Relations between the Emperor, the Chancellor and the Reichstag

William II sided with the army in the Zabern episode, refusing as its commander in chief to criticise it in any way. At no point in the entire controversy did he consult his Chancellor, Bethmann-Hollweg, bypassing him completely and showing him to be largely powerless in matters relating to the armed forces.

Also revealed to be powerless was the Reichstag. The Reichstag censured Bethmann-Hollweg and demanded his resignation but the Emperor simply ignored its demands. The Reichstag was seen to be unable to impose its will on the government, even in circumstances in which it had public opinion on its side and the government was seeking to defend the indefensible.

Divisions in German society

The Zabern incident exposed the fault lines dividing German society. On one side were the democrats – the Left Liberals and the Social Democrats. On the other were the authoritarians – the Kaiser, the army, the *Junkers*, the right-wing pressure groups. In 1914 these two Germanies were deadlocked: the democrats failed to establish the principle of government accountability to the Reichstag, but the authoritarians accepted that a military coup aimed at depriving the Reichstag of its law-making powers was out of the question.

'It was as if a flashlight had lit up for a moment the deep and ever-deepening divisions within German politics.'

Volker Berghahn on the Zabern incident, *Imperial Germany 1871–1918*, published by Berghahn Books 2005

Domestic politics 1900–14 timeline

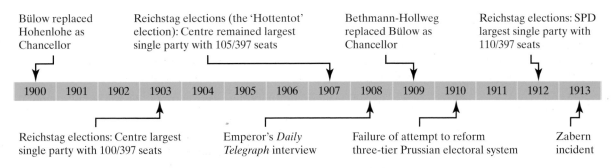

Bülow replaced Hohenlohe as Chancellor

Reichstag elections (the 'Hottentot' election): Centre remained largest single party with 105/397 seats

Bethmann-Hollweg replaced Bülow as Chancellor

Reichstag elections: SPD largest single party with 110/397 seats

1900 1901 1902 1903 1904 1905 1906 1907 1908 1909 1910 1911 1912 1913

Reichstag elections: Centre largest single party with 100/397 seats

Emperor's *Daily Telegraph* interview

Failure of attempt to reform three-tier Prussian electoral system

Zabern incident

Two views of the Zabern incident

'The events in Zabern have developed into an enormous scandal. This is due to our extraordinary constitution, according to which the Imperial Chancellor, the highest official of the Empire, is entirely powerless in the face of the military. He cannot even force the suspension of the youngest lieutenant. Our military is entirely independent, a separate power in the State. Within our semi-absolutist government there exists then an entirely absolutist institution – militarism.' (From Vorwärts, SPD newspaper, 1913)	'The army has only done its plain duty. The Zabern incident has been maliciously exaggerated by newspapers given to agitation. The garrison at Zabern acted under systematically organized provocation. Both officers and men conducted themselves as Germans expected their soldiers to do. Without the army there would not be a stone in place in Germany today.' (Falkenhayn, Prussian War Minister, speaking in the Reichstag, 1913)

The impact of the First World War

The *Burgfrieden*, 1914

By now, Germany was at war. In Germany, as in other combatant countries, the outbreak of war was followed by a setting-aside of domestic political differences. Germany's political truce was known as the *Burgfrieden* (literally, the 'fortress peace').

Essential notes

The controversy surrounding the extent of Germany's responsibility for the outbreak of the First World War is examined in the next chapter.

- All political parties voted (August 1914) for war credits – to authorise the government to raise money for the war effort by selling bonds to the German public.

- Political parties undertook not to criticise the government in wartime.

- The trades unions promised to refrain from strike action during the war.

It was not a foregone conclusion that the SPD would support the war. Before 1914 it had repeatedly proclaimed its opposition to militarism and imperialism. There were a number of reasons why it did not stand by its anti-war principles in 1914:

Examiners' notes

You will not be asked questions on the purely military aspects of the First World War. Focus attention on the impact of the conflict on the domestic political situation, in particular, on the dramatic developments of 1918.

- The SPD leaders and supporters were patriots. 'We will not desert our Fatherland in its hour of need,' declared Hugo Haase, left-wing chairman of the SPD, in August 1914.

- The SPD accepted government assurances that Germany had been forced into fighting a defensive war.

- There was a hope that loyalty would be rewarded by political concessions such as reform of the three-tier Prussian franchise.

Military aspects of the war

On the Eastern Front: Germany:
- defeated Russia in the battles of Tannenberg and the Masurian Lakes in 1914
- advanced into Russian Poland in 1915; withstood the 'Brusilov Offensive' in 1916
- advanced deeper into Russian territory in 1915; made huge territorial gains under the Treaty of Brest-Litovsk (March 1918).

On the Western Front:
- the failure of the Schlieffen Plan led to a military stalemate, which lasted until the Armistice (November 1918)
- The Allies imposed a naval blockade on Germany in 1914. German merchant ships were seized and neutral ships searched for cargo destined for Germany. This operation succeeded in its aim to restrict the flow of food and raw materials into Germany. The blockade was not lifted until July 1919.

Essential notes

German military casualties 1914–18:

- 1.6 million killed
- 1.6 million seriously wounded
- 2.2 million otherwise wounded.

Breakdown of the *Burgfrieden,* 1914–17

The national unity of 1914 was short-lived. A number of factors eroded popular support for the war:

- There was a rising number of casualties.

- There were acute shortages of food and consumer goods, largely resulting from the Allied blockade. Food shortages were at their worst in the 'turnip winter' of 1916–17, when Germany's difficulties were compounded by a failure of the potato crop. Hunger and malnutrition were widespread. Food rationing (introduced 1915) did little to help.

- There was a fall in real wages of around 30% as a result of inflation. The principal cause of inflation was the government's policy of paying for the war by printing money.

- The passing of the Auxiliary Labour Law (1916), which gave the government the power to conscript civilian workers aged 16–60 and decide where they should work. This measure was deeply resented within the working class.

- There was no equality of sacrifice. While the lower classes experienced hardship, the *Junkers* clung to their tax privileges and until 1916 companies paid no tax on their war profits.

The crisis of 1917

In 1916–17, with Germany having failed, after more than two years' fighting, to land a knock-out blow, army chiefs and their political allies successfully pushed for an intensification of the war effort:

- Hard-line generals came to the fore: in August 1916 Hindenburg replaced Falkenhayn as army chief of staff with Ludendorff as his nominal deputy. Both were intent on waging 'total war'.

- The Hindenburg Programme, an ambitious scheme to double munitions production by militarising the economy, was launched in August 1916. Note that the Auxiliary Labour Law (see above) was part of the Hindenburg Programme.

- In February 1917 Germany embarked on unrestricted submarine warfare (attacking neutral ships trading with the Triple *Entente*), gambling that its enemies would be brought to their knees before outrage over the sinking of American ships brought the USA into the war.

The army's high command and its political allies failed to mobilise popular opinion behind their 'total war' approach. By mid-1917, support for the war on the political left and in the political centre was clearly waning:

- There was a sharp increase in the number of strikes.

- The SPD split, with left-wing, anti-war elements breaking away to form the Independent Social Democratic Party (USPD) in April 1917.

- The Reichstag Peace Resolution was passed in July 1917.

Against this background, pre-war political divisions re-emerged with a vengeance. Infuriated conservatives condemned socialist critics of the war as defeatists and enemies of the Reich. They also turned their fire on Bethmann-Hollweg, who wanted to preserve the *Burgfrieden* by making concessions to the left (in particular, by reforming the Prussian electoral system). The high command forced his resignation (July 1917). By this time William II had been marginalised politically. In the later stages of the war Hindenburg and Ludendorff were virtual dictators.

Examiners' notes

You need to be clear about the social and economic effects of the war and about the ways in which these contributed to mounting opposition to the war and increasing polarisation of opinion within Germany. The mood of national unity of 1914 faded, and by 1918 it had disappeared.

Essential notes

The Reichstag Peace Resolution was a thinly veiled plea for the opening of peace negotiations with the Allies. It called for 'a peace of understanding and a lasting reconciliation of peoples', but added that Germany would fight on if the Allies refused to agree to such a peace. Backed by most members of the SPD, the Centre Party and the Progressive People's Party, the resolution was passed 212–126.

Examiners' notes

Attention should be given to the reasons the revolution(s) of late 1918 took place, and to the reasons German society in 1918 was even more deeply divided than it had been in 1914.

Kaiserreich to republic: the November Revolution, 1918

Imperial Germany was overthrown by a 'popular revolution' that took place in November 1918. This 'popular revolution' was preceded by the so-called 'revolution from above' – an unsuccessful (and cynical) attempt by the army high command to turn Germany into a constitutional monarchy.

The 'revolution from above', October 1918

October 1918: the 'revolution from above'
The army high command, acting largely out of self-interest, tried to impose constitutional reform on Germany from above

November 1918: the 'popular revolution'
Socialists took control of Germany's major cities: moderate socialists proclaimed the existence of a democratic republic

In March 1918 fighting on the Eastern Front ended when the Treaty of Brest–Litovsk was imposed on defeated Russia. This enabled Germany to transfer more than half a million men to the Western Front and launch a major offensive designed to achieve a decisive breakthrough before American forces arrived on the battlefield in large numbers. The 'Ludendorff Offensive' failed. In autumn 1918 the German high command (though not the general public) realised the war was lost.

In these circumstances Hindenburg and Ludendorff had two aims: to secure the best possible peace terms and to protect the reputation of the German army. In pursuit of these aims they urged William II to appoint a government consisting of representatives of the largest parties in the Reichstag – which meant turning the German Empire at a stroke into a parliamentary democracy. One of their calculations was that a democratic Germany might be more leniently treated in peace talks than one seen as militarist and authoritarian. Another calculation was that blame for Germany's defeat could be off-loaded from the army onto civilian politicians.

William II reluctantly agreed to the high command's proposals. The new Chancellor was Prince Max of Baden, widely respected as head of the German Red Cross but a political lightweight. The most important figures in the new government were Philip Scheidemann (SPD) and Matthias Erzberger (Centre Party).

The Allies were unconvinced by Germany's last-minute conversion to democracy. They made it known they would not open cease-fire talks with Germany while William II continued to occupy a position of authority of any kind. Inside Germany, calls for the Emperor's abdication – from his war-weary subjects – grew louder.

The high command wanted the appearance of democracy but had no intention of surrendering its own power and freedom of action. It treated the new government with contempt. Its attitude was typified by Admiral

Essential notes

A militarist society is one in which military values are glorified and in which military leaders possess undue political influence.

Authoritarianism is a form of government in which rule is imposed on people without their consent. Authoritarian governments are typically quick to resort to intimidation and force if challenged.

Scheer, chief of the German naval staff who, in late October 1918, ordered a last-minute suicide attack on the British navy without seeking any kind of clearance from his political superiors.

The 'popular revolution', November 1918

Scheer's arrogance triggered the next phase of the German revolution. The sailors of Germany's High Seas fleet refused to take part in a suicide mission. Instead they seized control of the naval base at Kiel on the Baltic and proceeded to set up an elected council of sailors and workers (or 'soviet') to run it.

Other towns and cities followed where Kiel had led. Soviets were set up in Hamburg, Cologne, Frankfurt, Munich and Berlin. The army made no attempt to intervene. By 9 November the whole of Germany was effectively in the hands of soviets controlled by supporters of the MSPD and the smaller USPD. 9 November was a day of high drama. There were three key developments:

- William II bowed to the inevitable and abdicated.

- Prince Max's coalition government, recognising that Germany's socialists were now in the driving seat, resigned; in its place came a six-man provisional government consisting of three members of the MSPD and three from the USPD with Friedrich Ebert at its head.

- Philip Schiedemann, a senior figure in the MSPD, proclaimed the existence of a German Republic.

The army and big business, November 1918

As the *Kaiserreich* was collapsing, Germany's conservative elites scrambled to safeguard their interests by negotiating with those now in power – that is, with people they had previously described as 'enemies of the Fatherland'. The army reached an agreement with the MSPD and the employers with the trades union movement.

Essential notes

The term MSPD (Majority Social Democrats) is used to refer to the main body of the Social Democratic Party in the period between the USPD's breakaway in 1917 and its disbandment in 1922.

Army: The Ebert–Groener Pact 9 November 1918	Big Business: The Stinnes–Legien Agreement 9–12 November 1918
The army high command undertook to support government efforts to combat 'Bolshevism' in return for a government promise to do what it could to preserve discipline in the army. Groener had succeeded Ludendorff as the army's deputy chief of staff in late 1918.	Germany's employers agreed to introduce an eight-hour day (a demand they had long resisted) in return for union promises to prevent disruption in the mines and factories. Hugo Stinnes was a Ruhr industrial tycoon and Carl Legien a prominent Social Democratic trade unionist.

Armistice, 11 November 1918

Formal cease-fire talks began under Prince Max's government on 7 November. The German delegation was headed by the Centre Party leader Matthias Erzberger. There were no negotiations as such: Germany had no alternative but to agree to Allied proposals. The Armistice came into effect on 11 November.

Examiners' notes

Making judgements about the extent of Germany's responsibility for the outbreak of the First World War requires not only knowledge and understanding of German policy-making but also awareness of the broader international context within which Germany acted. This includes an awareness of the interests and policies of other Great Powers.

The European Great Powers and their interests

The European Great Powers

International affairs in the early 20th century largely revolved around relations between the European 'Great Powers'. There were disparities among these powers in terms of size and strength (still, none of them dwarfed the others in the way that the USA and the Soviet Union did in 1945–90).

The Great Powers in 1914: economic and military strength (population and army strength in millions; steel production in millions of tons; Dreadnought figures relate to number of ships in service)

Britain

Population	46 m
Steel production	7.7 m
Army: peacetime strength	0.25 m
Army reserves	0.4 m
Navy: Dreadnoughts	19

Germany

Population	67 m
Steel production	17.6 m
Army: peacetime strength	0.9 m
Army reserves	3 m
Navy: Dreadnoughts	13

Russia

Population	167 m
Steel production	4.8 m
Army: peacetime strength	1.4 m
Army reserves	5.1 m
Navy: Dreadnoughts	4

France

Population	40 m
Steel production	4.6 m
Army: peacetime strength	0.9 m
Army reserves	2.9 m
Navy: Dreadnoughts	8

Great Britain

Russia

Germany

France

Austria-Hungary

Italy

Italy

Population	36 m
Steel production	0.1 m
Army: peacetime strength	0.3 m
Army reserves	1 m
Navy: Dreadnoughts	1

Spain

Austrian Empire

Population	49 m
Steel production	2.6 m
Army: peacetime strength	0.4 m
Army reserves	1.4 m
Navy: Dreadnoughts	2

Russia was the most populous of the Great Powers but in 1914 population size was not as important a determinant of military power as it had been in the past because, in the course of the 19th century, warfare had been revolutionised by technology. By the early 20th century, a country's military strength depended largely on its capacity to equip its forces with sophisticated weaponry – which meant that much hinged on the size and quality of its industrial base. Here Germany was better placed than any of the other Great Powers. Its steel output in 1914 was more than double that of its nearest competitor and its engineering prowess meant that its armaments factories, such as the gigantic Krupps munitions complex at Essen in the Ruhr, could churn out vast quantities of high-quality artillery, machine guns and breech-loading rifles.

Austria and Italy were the least consequential of the Great Powers.

Britain was the pre-eminent naval power but, with only a small army by continental European standards, was a relatively insignificant land power. Other European Great Powers did not regard Britain as a key player in purely continental affairs.

Aims and interests of the European Great Powers in the late 19th century

France
France's defeat by Prussia in 1870–1 and the consequent loss of Alsace-Lorraine left it thirsting for '*la revanche*' (revenge). However, the widening gap between France and Germany in economic and demographic terms meant that it was not in a position to take on Germany alone. The principal objective of French diplomacy after 1871 was therefore to find a heavyweight ally.

Essential notes

The breech-loading rifle, which came into widespread use in the 1860s, replaced the musket, over which it had several advantages, including greater accuracy and ease of reloading.

Rifled artillery firing conical shells with great accuracy over long distances replaced cannon from the 1860s onwards.

The first machine gun (the 'Gatling gun') came into use in 1861.

Source 1
(From Paul Kennedy, *The Rise and Fall of the Great Powers*, published by Random House 1988)

Two factors ensured that the rise of Imperial Germany would have a more substantial impact on the Great Power balance than either of its fellow 'newcomer' states, Japan and Italy. The first was that Germany had arisen right in the centre of the European states system: its very creation had directly impinged on the interests of Austria-Hungary and France, and its existence had altered the relative position of all of the existing Great Powers of Europe. The second factor was the sheer speed and extent of Germany's growth in industrial, commercial and military/naval terms. By the eve of the First World War its national power was not only three or four times Italy's and Japan's, it was well ahead of France and Russia and had probably overtaken Britain as well. Germany was the most powerful state in Europe, and still growing. This alone was to make 'the German question' the epicentre of so much of world politics for more than half a century after 1890.

Examiners' notes

Note the different elements that the sources you will have to analyse in Section B might contain – a *claim or interpretation* (Source 1 claims that the emergence of Germany had a bigger impact on international affairs than that of either Italy or Japan), *reasons* offered in support of claim (Source 1 points to Germany's geographical location and its economic and military strength) and *evidence* offered in support of the claim or reasons (Source 1 compares Germany's national power in 1914 with that of other Great Powers).

☞ Continued on the next two pages

Essential notes

Otto von Bismarck was Imperial Chancellor, 1871–90. During this period he was the principal architect of German domestic and foreign policy.

Examiners' notes

Questions will not be set that draw on events before 1900, but some understanding of them is necessary to explain international relations from 1900.

Essential notes

'The Eastern Question' is a term used to describe issues and disputes that arose out of the decline of the Turkish Empire and over what arrangements would be put in place in the event of its collapse.

Germany

Under Otto von Bismarck, 1871–90, Germany aimed to maintain peace and stability in Europe in order to concentrate on nation-building at home. The chief threat to stability was France. Germany therefore set out to keep France isolated – that is, to prevent it from acquiring allies. This entailed cultivating good relations with Russia and Austria so that they were kept out of France's clutches. German foreign policy before 1890 was low-key and risk-averse: after 1890 it became more belligerent and aggressive.

Austria

Austria was a declining power. It was a multinational state threatened with destruction by the demands for independence of the nationalities within it. Austria's foreign policy aims were self-preservation and the retention of great power status.

Austria's most pressing external problem arose out of its acquisition in 1878 of Bosnia and Herzegovina, formerly provinces of the Turkish Empire. These provinces had a complicated ethnicity but contained a large number of Serbs. To the east of Bosnia-Herzegovina lay the independent state of Serbia, which aimed to incorporate the Bosnian Serbs into a unified Serbian super-state – and to this end backed separatist movements within Bosnia-Herzegovina. Serbia's ambitions thus put it on a collision course with Austria. Austria was not, however, in a position to crush Serbia by force, because Serbia had a powerful protector and ally in the shape of Russia.

Russia

Late 19th-century Russia was an expansionist power. It aimed to expand in the Far East at the expense of the ramshackle Chinese Empire and to extend its influence in south-eastern Europe (the Balkans) at the expense of the decaying Turkish Empire. The great prize Russia sought in south-eastern Europe was control of the straits connecting the Black Sea to the Mediterranean.

In order to further its aims in south-east Europe, Russia posed as the patron and protector of Serbia, with which it had (or so it claimed) ties of religion and ethnicity. Russia's patronage of Serbia brought it into conflict with Austria, Serbia's enemy. The antagonism that developed between Russia and Austria made it extremely difficult for Germany to keep on good terms with both.

Britain

Britain's main concern in the late 19th century was fending off threats to its colonial possessions around the world. The principal threats came from France (in Africa) and Russia (in Asia).

Britain wanted to avoid the situation in Europe whereby the continent was dominated by a single power. This was because a single dominant power would possess a springboard from which it could invade Britain and would also have the ability to close the continent to British trade. However, if no power was seen to be making a bid for supremacy Britain had no reason to involve itself in European affairs.

Italy

Italy was the weakest of the Great Powers. In European affairs it was hostile to France, which it saw as a rival for influence in the Mediterranean. Italy also sought colonies, seeing possession of a colonial empire as a symbol of great power status.

In 1882 Italy's hostility towards France led it to inquire about the possibility of associating itself with the Austro–German alliance, sometimes called the Dual Alliance. Bismarck was willing to oblige, seeing Italy as a useful, if modest, addition to his line-up against France: the Dual Alliance thus became the Triple Alliance.

1890 was a turning-point in German foreign policy. Source 2 offers an explanation of how and why:

> **Source 2**
> (From Norman Stone, *World War One: A Short History*, published by Allen Lane 2007)
>
> The confidence of Germans increased as the country's industry boomed, and success went to their heads. Bismarck had been cautious. He could see that a strong Germany might unite her neighbours against her. But a new generation was coming up, and it was full of itself. The symbolic figure at its head was a new young emperor, Kaiser Wilhelm II, who came to the throne in 1888. His model was England. She was vastly rich and had an enormous overseas empire. Why should not Germany acquire an overseas empire to match? Under Wilhelm I, German power, and the blundering expression of it became a … European problem.

Essential notes

Russia and the Balkan region were both strongholds of the Orthodox branch of Christianity.

Essential notes

It was widely assumed in the late 19th century that the inhabitants of Russia and Eastern Europe, including the Balkans, belonged to a distinctive ethnic group – the Slavs.

Examiners' notes

Each Section B question is accompanied by three sources that differ in their interpretations of the relevant controversy. To make the best use of these sources, first establish the interpretation that is being offered. For example, in Source 2, Stone suggests that Germany became a disruptive force in European affairs in the 1890s and 1900s as a result of the arrogance of the post-Bismarck generation.

Essential notes

Bülow was one of the foremost advocates of *Weltpolitik*. In 1897 he told the Reichstag: 'we also demand our place in the sun' – that is, overseas colonies.

Essential notes

German gains of territory as a result of post-1890 *Weltpolitik* were extremely limited:

- Heligoland (1890)
- Kiachow, a trading base in China (1897)
- Samoa, the Marianas Islands and the Caroline Islands (all in the Pacific) (1899)
- A small area of land in central Africa given by France as compensation for the French takeover in Morocco (1911).

Essential notes

The principal advocate of naval expansion was Admiral Alfred von Tirpitz, head of the German Imperial Naval Office (1897–1916). Tirpitz argued that a formidable navy was essential if Germany was to become a genuine world power. He called for a fleet consisting of heavy battleships designed to operate in the North Sea. The intentions were to pressure Britain into supporting German colonial policy and to make Germany an attractive alliance prospect to other Great Powers.

Weltpolitik and *Flottenpolitik*

Colonies and *Weltpolitik*

Germany first acquired overseas possessions under Bismarck. In 1884–5 Togo, Cameroon, south-west Africa, Tanganyika and part of New Guinea (in the Pacific) became German colonies. Bismarck, however, was not a fervent imperialist. He had no empire-building master plan. His motives for joining the 'scramble for Africa' were political (to win support at home) and diplomatic (to give himself a bargaining counter in his dealings with France). European affairs remained his overriding priority.

In the 1890s this Europe-centred diplomacy was superseded by *Weltpolitik*. *Weltpolitik* literally means 'world policy', but should be understood as a shorthand term used to refer to Germany's aim of building a colonial empire and, by doing so, transforming itself into a world power, as opposed to a purely European power. *Weltpolitik* was an aspiration rather than a clearly defined programme. There was no detailed plan to win control of specific pieces of territory. However, Germany's pursuit of *Weltpolitik* had important consequences for its relations with other powers, especially Britain, and as such was a significant turning-point in international affairs.

Reasons for the pursuit of *Weltpolitik*

- *Weltpolitik* owed much to considerations of status and prestige. To many conservative and middle-class Germans it appeared that the country's military prowess and growing economic strength called for the achievement of recognition as a power of world importance.

- Note, too, that the pre-war German ruling class was heavily influenced by Social Darwinist ideas. Social Darwinism held that nations were the same as biological species, competing against each other in a struggle for existence in which only the fittest would survive. Only by becoming a world power, it was claimed, could Germany compete effectively against world powers such as Britain.

- *Weltpolitik* was also pursued for reasons of domestic politics. Conservatives hoped that empire-building would rally the middle classes behind the *Kaiserreich* and marginalise the Social Democrats.

- Right-wing pressure groups such as the Colonial Society made out an economic case for empire-building. Colonies, it was argued, could be a source of raw materials and offer a market for German exports.

Flottenpolitik

Flottenpolitik literally means 'fleet policy' but should be understood to refer to the expansion of the German navy after the passage of the 1898 Naval Law.

Before 1898 Germany's navy was a small coastal force with no heavy battleships.

Naval expansion was popular with the German middle classes. The navy was seen as a properly German institution (not a Prussian one like the army) which had officers who were solid professionals (unlike the over-privileged *Junkers* who dominated the upper ranks of the army).

Source 3
(From James Joll, *The Origins of the First World War*, published by Pearson Education 2007)

Although Tirpitz was principally concerned with the creation of a navy for its own sake and as a means of achieving a not very clearly defined position as a world power, he was also aware of the role the navy might play in providing a new rallying-point for German opinion. He hoped that naval building would favour an authoritarian system of government at home while abroad tipping the balance of power in Germany's favour.

Source 4
(From A.J.P. Taylor, *The Course of German History*, published by Methuen & Co. Ltd 1961)

Tirpitz fell back constantly on the argument that a great navy was an essential possession of a Great Power. Bethmann-Hollweg declared that a German navy was necessary 'for the general purposes of imperial greatness'. The political effect of the naval programme was far-reaching. It won the enthusiastic support of the great steel monopolies who were its direct beneficiaries. Yet this interest-policy could be presented to the German electors as a 'national' policy.

Consequences of *Weltpolitik* and *Flottenpolitik*: the emergence of Anglo–German antagonism

- Before *Flottenpolitik* there were no strong reasons for Anglo–German enmity. Germany's interest lay in Europe: Britain's outside Europe. Relations between the two countries were friendly but distant.

- *Flottenpolitik* was key to the development of Anglo–German antagonism. Britain assumed that it was faced with a bid to dislodge it from its position as the world's pre-eminent naval and imperial power. It was determined to out-build and see off its challenger. A naval arms race ensued.

- Technological change gave the Anglo–German naval race its special intensity. Germany started from a long way behind Britain, so far as old-style battleships were concerned, but in 1906 Britain launched *HMS Dreadnought*, first of a new type of battleship. Britain and Germany started building Dreadnoughts from a position of near parity. This led to a 'naval panic' in Britain in 1908–9.

- As Anglo–German hostility became more intense, British suspicions of Germany widened. By 1908 Britain's foreign policy-makers had convinced themselves that Germany was not only seeking to establish itself as a world power at Britain's expense but was also intent on dominating continental Europe. This was Britain's worst foreign policy nightmare: a great power aiming both to dominate Europe and to challenge Britain in the wider world.

Examiners' notes

In your analysis of the Section B sources you need to be sensitive to the extent of agreement between sources. Here Joll (Source 3) and Taylor (Source 4) agree that one of the motives of those responsible for the naval building programme was a desire to increase national prestige, but they disagree on other motives: Joll argues that naval building was designed to rally support for *Kaiserreich* inside Germany, while Taylor sees it as a concession to industrial interests.

Essential notes

Before the *Dreadnought*, battleships carried guns of different sizes, but the *Dreadnought* carried only heavy guns. The *Dreadnought* was also faster and better armoured than earlier battleships.

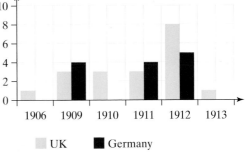

The Anglo–German naval race: number of Dreadnoughts completed each year before 1914

UK   Germany

Examiners' notes

It will help you to express yourself clearly and concisely in the examination if you have a command of the terminology used to describe relations between states.

Essential notes

Treaty: a written agreement between states, which can be about any issue.

Alliance: a written agreement between two or more states involving a commitment to go to war together in specified circumstances.

Entente: an informal understanding between states to work together in foreign affairs.

Rapprochement: a coming-together of states that have previously been hostile.

Ultimatum: a demand by one state on another, backed by the threat of war or other penalties in the event of non-compliance.

The European alliance system before 1914

The Triple Alliance

The Triple Alliance was not an association of equal partners. Both Austria and Italy were massively inferior to Germany in terms of military power.

When he established the Dual Alliance in 1879, it was not Bismarck's intention to tie Germany permanently to Austria. Yet the alliance with Austria was regularly renewed and became the cornerstone of German foreign policy. Germany's commitment to Austria owed much to fears that its collapse would create a dangerous power vacuum in central and south-eastern Europe from which Russia was likely to benefit.

The Austro–German alliance was originally a defensive one: each promised to go to war alongside the other in the event of it being attacked by Russia. In the years before 1914, however, its character changed and it became more of an offensive arrangement. In the Bosnian crisis (1908), Austria and Germany collaborated to inflict a diplomatic humiliation on Russia. After the Bosnian crisis the two countries made joint war plans for the first time: in the event of conflict Germany would attack France and Austria would launch an offensive into Russian Poland.

The Franco–Russian alliance, 1894

In 1890 Bismarck's successors decided not to renew Germany's Reinsurance Treaty with Russia. They did not share his view that Germany's security depended on a complicated balancing act involving Russia and Austria.

- Scenting an opportunity to secure a heavyweight ally, France started to woo a now-isolated Russia.

- France and Russia became allies in 1894. Both committed themselves to support the other in the event of an attack by Germany.

- Remember that the Franco–Russian alliance was in some respects an unlikely one: Russia was a monarchy, France a republic; Russia was an autocracy, France a democracy.

- The Franco–Russian alliance left Germany open to the nightmare prospect of a *Zweifrontenkrieg* – a war on two fronts.

Britain's movement into the Franco–Russian orbit

In the early 20th century Britain ended its 'splendid isolation' from European affairs by aligning itself with France and Russia against Germany.

Britain was unwilling to enter into formal alliances with France and Russia because it wanted to retain freedom of manoeuvre. However, Anglo–French military conversations took place (from 1906 onwards), which gave rise to understandings about the deployment of British troops in France in the event of war against Germany. In the Anglo–French naval agreement (1912) Britain effectively promised to defend France's north coast against German attack.

The foundations of the Anglo–French and Anglo–Russian *ententes* were laid by the colonial agreements of 1904 and 1907.

Source 5
(From David Thomson, *Europe since Napoleon*, published by Penguin 1966)

The aim of Britain and France was to restore in Europe a balance of power less favourable to Germany. When, after 1907, Britain cast its lot with France and Russia, French and Russian military expansion offset German, British naval expansion offset German – and the feverish competition between the two camps achieved a remarkable equalisation of power and potential in Europe. The frightening feature of the rival alliances by 1914 was their rigidity and reliability. Each succeeding international crisis tightened the ties within each group.

How stable were the European alliances before 1914?

Bear in mind that the pre-1914 European alliances were not as fixed and rigid as they might appear:

- There were close dynastic links between Germany and Russia (William II and Nicholas II were cousins) and an influential pro-German, anti-French party at the Russian court. This left the French in fear of reconciliation between Germany and Russia, leaving them isolated.

- Many supporters of Britain's Liberal government were opposed to a close relationship with Tsarist Russia and favoured an attempt at Anglo–German *rapprochement*.

- Neither Germany nor Austria had any illusions about Italy's reliability as an ally.

The *Entente Cordiale* 1904 – Britain goes off with France, Germany feigns indifference

Examiners' notes

Section B questions require you to integrate the interpretations offered by the sources with your own knowledge of different interpretations of the controversy. Source 5 argues that the European alliance blocs became increasingly rigid in the years before 1914. You could use your own knowledge of the major pre-1914 international crises to support this claim or, alternatively, your own knowledge of tensions within the alliance blocs to challenge it.

Essential notes

In 1905 William II met Nicholas II in secret at Björkö (Finland) and persuaded him to agree to an alliance with Germany. Nicholas's horrified ministers persuaded him to go back on what he had done.

European diplomacy, 1900–14

Diplomatic developments 1900–14 in outline

Event	What happened?	Significance
Anglo–Japanese alliance, 1902	Both agreed to remain neutral if the other went to war with a third power and to fight together in the event of a wider war.	Allowed Britain to scale down its naval presence in the Far East and to concentrate naval resources in home waters.
Anglo–French agreement, 1904	Britain allowed France a free hand in Morocco in return for French acceptance of British control in Egypt.	Gave rise to the Anglo–French *entente* and marked the start of Britain's movement into the Franco–Russian orbit.
Russo–Japanese War, 1904–5	Russia was heavily defeated by Japan in a war arising out of the ambitions both had in China.	Prompted major reform of Russia's armed forces – a development that alarmed Germany.
First Morocco crisis, 1905–6	France wanted control over independent Morocco in order to safeguard its position in Algeria (French colony). William II triggered the crisis by landing at Tangier (1905) and pledging to support Moroccan independence. The dispute was referred to at an international conference (Algeciras, 1906), which sided with France, allowing it substantial – but not full – control of Morocco.	Germany provoked the crisis in order to destroy the Anglo–French *entente*. It believed that Britain would not stand by France and the French would conclude that Britain's friendship was worthless. However, Britain backed France and the *entente* was strengthened, not weakened. Britain's suspicions of German intentions were intensified.
Anglo–Russian agreement, 1907	Britain and Russia settled their disputes in central Asia (over Persia, Afghanistan and Tibet).	Gave rise to an Anglo–Russian *entente* and effectively created the Triple *Entente*.
Bosnian crisis, 1908	Austria annexed Bosnia-Herzegovina, despite the 1878 agreement that the provinces were to be controlled by Austria without becoming part of it.	Annexation was strongly opposed by Russia, but Germany weighed in strongly on Austria's side, forcing Russia to climb down. Russia was left bruised and resentful.
Second Morocco crisis, 1911	France moved towards a full takeover of Morocco. Germany demanded compensation, sending the *Panther* to Agadir to reinforce its demand. Britain intervened, warning Germany it was risking war.	Another failure to undermine the Anglo–French *entente* – though Germany did win compensation (land in central Africa). The forcefulness of Britain's intervention showed how far Anglo–German relations had deteriorated.
Balkan Wars, 1912–14	In the first war (1912–13) Bulgaria, Serbia, Greece and Montenegro set out, with Russian backing, to force Turkey out of its remaining territory in south-east Europe. In the second war (1913), the victorious Balkan states fought among themselves.	The first war led to a confrontation between Austria and Russia over the former's determination to restrict Serbia's gains: Germany and Britain restrained their respective partners.

German diplomacy before 1914: aggressive or defensive?

The assumption within the Triple *Entente* before 1914 was that Germany was intent upon world power and hegemony (domination) in Europe. These aims, it was claimed, were reflected in a foreign policy that was provocative and aggressive. Germany, by contrast, maintained that its diplomacy was forced upon it by *Entente* 'encirclement'.

Source 6

(From Immanuel Geiss, 'Origins of the First World War' in H.W. Koch (editor), *The Origins of the First Word War*, published by Macmillan 1972)

The effect of the German diplomatic defeat in the second Moroccan crisis was dramatic: German propaganda, from now on, loudly proclaimed that the Reich was 'encircled' by the *Entente* Powers, by a coalition of envious and mischievous Powers who were only waiting for their chance to overwhelm the Triple Alliance.

The German fear of 'encirclement' was mistaken – and there are reasons to doubt whether the German leaders themselves believed in the 'fairy tale' of encirclement. At least some of them seemed to realise that the *Entente* Powers had no aggressive intentions. Those Germans who sincerely believed in the threat constituted by 'encirclement' – and this was the overwhelming majority – clearly misunderstood the intentions of the *Entente*.

Arguments for regarding German diplomacy before 1914 as aggressive

- In the major pre-war diplomatic crises, Germany took the initiative, as opposed to reacting to initiatives taken by others. It is hard to see this approach as purely defensive.

- The first Morocco crisis began with a high-profile intervention by William II in a matter in which no vital German interest was at stake. The only plausible interpretation of German policy in 1905 is that it was a calculated attempt to raise the diplomatic temperature and drive a wedge between Britain and France.

- In the 1908–9 Bosnian crisis, Germany took the opportunity to inflict a diplomatic humiliation on a Russia weakened by its defeat in the Russo–Japanese war of 1904–5. German policy was ill-judged in that it succeeded only in leaving Russia resentful and determined to avoid any further humiliation at Germany's hands.

- The second Morocco crisis, like the first, was initiated by an intervention far more dramatic than anything the circumstances warranted. Britain, not unreasonably, was quick to draw the conclusion that Germany had an ulterior motive – weakening the Anglo–French *entente*.

Examiners' notes

You will be required to evaluate the interpretations presented in the Section B sources. Evaluation involves making a judgement about the persuasiveness of an interpretation. You need to take a number of considerations into account when making your judgement:

1. Does the source itself offer any reasoning or evidence in support of the interpretation it offers? In Source 6, for instance, the assertion that some of Germany's political leaders accepted that the *Entente* powers had no aggressive intent is not supported by any specific examples.

2. Do the other sources corroborate or challenge the interpretation offered in the source you are evaluating?

3. Does your own knowledge corroborate or challenge the interpretation offered in the source you are evaluating?

Continued on the next two pages

German diplomacy before 1914 was certainly clumsy and provocative – but note that this is not by itself proof that Germany was aiming at European hegemony, still less that it was intent on war.

Arguments in defence of German diplomacy before 1914

- Germany was not alone in behaving provocatively before 1914: British policy in the second Morocco crisis was extremely forceful, and Russia displayed a readiness to take risks when it backed the Balkan states in the war of 1912.

- Germany's flamboyant interventions in the two Morocco crises may very well have owed something to a wish to impress public opinion at home.

- It would be wrong to assume that Germany's foreign and defence policies before 1914 were highly coordinated and derived from a clear and agreed strategy: the Chancellor, the Foreign Office, the army and the Emperor each had their own views, and sometimes they differed. William II, for example, was doubtful about the wisdom of the speech his advisers persuaded him to make at Tangier in 1905, and he needed to be persuaded to authorise the despatch of the *Panther* to Agadir in 1911.

The July Crisis

The 'July Crisis' is a phrase used to describe the events that took place between 28 June, when the heir to the Austrian throne was murdered by a Bosnian Serb nationalist, and 4 August, when Britain, the last of the European powers to commit itself, declared war on Germany.

As a result of Sarajevo, Austria was itching for a showdown with Serbia but it could not act on its own. Any move against Serbia carried with it the near certainty of Russian intervention – and Austria was too weak to confront Russia. Austria therefore turned to its ally, Germany, for support and by so doing initiated the sequence of decisions that led to the outbreak of a general war (see diagram opposite).

Interpreting the July Crisis

In the July Crisis a localised dispute in the Balkans escalated into a general European war. It was not inevitable that this should happen. There had been numerous Austro–Russian clashes over the Balkans before 1914 and each of them had been contained. This raises the question of how and why the 1914 crisis differed from earlier crises. Historians have, broadly speaking, offered two different explanations.

There are those who argue that in 1914 decision-makers miscalculated (in other words, they made assumptions about the consequences of their actions that turned out to be mistaken). It might, for example, be argued that when Germany's leaders issued the 'blank cheque' (a promise of support whatever it chose to do) to Austria they mistakenly assumed that Russia would back down once it knew they intended to stand by their ally – much as it had done in the 1908–9 Bosnian crisis. Historians who argue that decision-makers miscalculated in July 1914 usually go on to argue that no one country was to blame for what happened.

Essential notes

The murder victim was Archduke Franz Ferdinand; the perpetrator was Gavrilo Princip; the murder took place in Sarajevo, capital of Bosnia.

Examiners' notes

The Specification requires you to be able to evaluate the view that Germany, like all the participants in the conflict, was the helpless prisoner of uncontrollable circumstances. Consider how far the mismanaged July Crisis accounts for the Great Powers tumbling into war in 1914.

The alternative explanation is that decision-makers – and in particular Germany's leaders – did not miscalculate but knew exactly what they were doing. On this interpretation, Germany's leaders at the very least knew when they gave the 'blank cheque' to Austria that there was a serious risk that a general European war would result. Some historians go further and maintain that it was Germany's intention throughout the crisis to force the issue and provoke a general war. Historians who accuse Germany's leaders of 'brinkmanship' – a readiness to go to the brink of war to further their ambitions – or of deliberate aggression, go on to argue that Germany was largely responsible for what happened in 1914.

The July Crisis: key decisions

5–6 July
Germany made the decision to back Austria whatever action it took against Serbia. The risk involved in giving Austria a 'blank cheque' – escalation of the Austro–Serbian dispute into a general war – was recognised and accepted. This was the most important decision of the July Crisis. There is no consensus among historians about the reasons that it was made.

7 July
Secure in the knowledge of German support, Austria decided to force the issue with Serbia by issuing it with a deliberately unacceptable ultimatum. Because of Austria's military unpreparedness, the ultimatum was not delivered until 23 July. Austria declared war on Serbia on 28 July after the rejection of its ultimatum.

28 July
The response of Russia to the Austrian ultimatum had been to promise Serbia support in public while urging caution in private. However, after the Austrian declaration of war, Russia decided on a partial mobilisation of its army. This was essentially a diplomatic move designed to persuade Austria to call off hostilities. Germany demanded a halt to Russian mobilisation: Russia responded by ordering full mobilisation on 30 July. Germany declared war on Russia on 1 August.

3 August
France decided to honour its alliance obligations to Russia. This decision was forced by Germany's demand – made before the declaration of war on Russia – that France remain neutral in the event of a Russo–German war and surrender fortresses on its border with Germany as a sign of its good faith. France refused. Germany declared war on France on 3 August.

4 August
Following Germany's declaration of war on Russia and France, Britain decided to join its Triple *Entente* partners and declared war on Germany. The decision was shaped more by fear of Germany than by loyalty to France and Russia. Germany's violation of Belgian neutrality was instrumental in rallying British public opinion behind the war.

Essential notes

Fritz Fischer (1908–99) produced two major works on the origins of the First World War in the 1960s: *Griff nach der Weltmacht* in 1961 (literally 'Grasping at world power', but published in English as *Germany's Aims in the First World War*) and *War of Illusions* in 1969.

Germany-blaming interpretations of the outbreak of the First World War

Origins

The debate on Germany's responsibility for the outbreak of war in 1914 began with the charge of 'war guilt' levelled at it in Article 231 of the Versailles Treaty. Germany rejected Article 231 and campaigned furiously against it. The campaign was successful: by the 1950s it had become widely accepted that responsibility for the outbreak of war in 1914 did not lie with Germany alone. This 'comfortable consensus' (Annika Mombauer, *The Origins of the First World War*, 2002) came to an end with the publication of Fritz Fischer's work in the 1960s.

The Fischer thesis

Fischer's interpretation of the outbreak of the First World War was a Germany-blaming one. He argued that Germany's leaders may not have been solely to blame for what happened in 1914 but bore a 'substantial share' of the responsibility for it.

Fischer's interpretation consists of a central thesis, or overall conclusion, and three main supporting arguments.

Fischer's interpretation

Overall conclusion
Germany's ruling class was determined to establish Germany as a world power and was ready to wage a war of aggression in order to achieve its objective.

Supporting argument	**Supporting argument**	**Supporting argument**
Before 1914 the German government was actively planning to achieve domination in Europe and to enlarge Germany's overseas empire.	Germany was intent on a general European war before 1914 and saw the Austro–Serbian crisis in 1914 as an unmissable opportunity to bring one about.	Members of Germany's ruling class, believing themselves to be facing a crisis at home that jeopardised their political future and foreign policy ambitions, saw war as a solution to their domestic problems.

Evidence
In September 1914 Bethmann-Hollweg drafted a statement of war aims (the 'September Programme'). Among the specific objectives it contained were:
- the elimination of France and Russia as independent Great Powers
- the establishment of a German-controlled economic bloc in central and eastern Europe (*Mitteleuropa*)
- the creation of a vast German colony straddling Central Africa.

Evidence
- At a meeting of the German Imperial War Council in December 1912, William II and others argued in favour of a war against Russia sooner rather than later.
- In July 1914 Germany gave Austria a 'blank cheque' to deal with Serbia knowing that this was likely to lead to a general European war.

Evidence
- The SPD became the largest single party in the Reichstag in 1912.
- The Zabern incident showed the army and ruling class in general to be unpopular.
- Further SPD gains in future elections could have made it difficult to pass the military budget.

Strengths and weaknesses of Fischer's interpretation

Fischer's interpretation gave rise to a heated debate among historians in Germany in the 1960s. It remains controversial. Fischer's interpretation has been influential in that few historians would now argue that Germany was no more to blame for the outbreak of war in 1914 than any of the other Great Powers. On the other hand, some of Fischer's specific claims have been widely criticised.

Strengths and weaknesses of Fischer's interpretation

Strengths

It was based on archival research: earlier interpretations of the outbreak of war in 1914 had been based on collections of printed sources.

It links Germany's *Weltpolitik*, its naval building programme, the belligerence of its pre-war diplomacy and its conduct in the July Crisis together in a coherent and plausible way.

It fits the known facts better than interpretations which suggest that Europe somehow stumbled into war in 1914.

Weaknesses

Fischer's critics challenge his view of the 1912 Imperial War Council and suggest that it did not in fact make a decision to go to war.

Fischer's critics point out that Bethmann-Hollweg's 'September Programme' was a statement of war aims written after the war had begun and insist that it cannot be taken as evidence of Germany's pre-war intentions. They add that the September Programme was the private musings of a single individual, not a formal expression of the policy of the government as a whole.

There is no conclusive evidence showing that Germany's leaders in 1914 were strongly influenced by domestic policy.

Preventive war

Fischer's claim that Germany deliberately launched a war of aggression in 1914 is what might be called a strong Germany-blaming interpretation of the outbreak of war. A less extreme, Germany-blaming interpretation is the view that in 1914 Germany embarked on a preventive war rather than a straightforward war of aggression.

The preventive war interpretation revolves around the claim that in 1914 Germany's leaders, in particular its army chiefs, were fearful of Russia's growing military power and wanted to eliminate the Russian threat before it was too late. There is no shortage of evidence that supports this view.

In 1904 the combined armies of Russia and France outnumbered those of Austria and Germany by 260 000; by 1914 the figure was over 1 million.

In the years before 1914 the military spending of the Triple *Entente* was much higher than that of the Triple Alliance.

In numerous surviving documents, prominent German political and military figures express concern about Russia's growing military power.

Essential notes

Historians who favour the 'preventive war' interpretation include Niall Ferguson in *The Pity of War* (1998):

The evidence points persuasively to a military 'first strike' designed to pre-empt a deterioration in Germany's military position – though this is by no means incompatible with the idea that the outcome of such a strike, if successful, would have been German mastery in Europe.

Essential notes

'Shared guilt' interpretations are sometimes called 'systemic' interpretations because they argue that the First World War arose out of one aspect or another of the pre-1914 international system – imperialism, *Realpolitik* or the influence of military plans.

'Shared guilt' interpretations of the outbreak of the First World War

'Shared guilt' interpretations of the outbreak of war in 1914 suggest that the European Great Powers were somehow collectively responsible for what happened. The view that one country was wholly or largely responsible is rejected. 'Shared guilt' interpretations are incompatible with Germany-blaming interpretations.

Marxist interpretations

Marxist writers argue that the origins of the First World War lay in imperialism. Lenin's views are not untypical. Imperialism, he claimed, was a by-product of late capitalism: the ruling class in all capitalist countries turned to expansion overseas as a means of making the profits needed to buy off increasingly militant workers at home. In these circumstances, he reasoned, conflict between imperialistic Great Powers was inevitable. Lenin's conclusion: 'The war was imperialistic – annexationist, predatory and plundering – on both sides' (*Imperialism*, 1916).

Lenin's theory was self-serving: it was designed to show that capitalism was on the point of collapse. But it does offer a useful reminder that Germany was not alone in being an expansionist power before 1914.

Essential notes

Realpolitik literally means 'realistic or practical politics', but is used to describe the view that foreign policy is essentially about the pursuit of self-interest and the exercise of power – leaving no room for ethical considerations such as fairness and honesty.

Liberal historians between the wars

German writers were not the only ones to deny German war guilt in the inter-war period. Liberal British and American historians such as G.P. Gooch, G.L. Dickinson and S.B. Fay did so too. These historians argued that the principal cause of war in 1914 was the *Realpolitik* practised by decision-makers in all of the Great Powers.

The basic assumption of *Realpolitik* is that states are obliged to compete against others for survival in an anarchic world. As a result, the argument runs, they adopt strategies designed to ensure their security and otherwise further their interests. These include making alliances with other states (to supplement their power) and building up their armed forces (to deter their enemies).

Examiners' notes

A major difficulty with 'shared guilt' interpretations is their refusal to apportion responsibility for the outbreak of war between the Great Powers in circumstances where there is evidence which suggests that some were intent on avoiding war and others were not.

Supporters of *Realpolitik* in the years before 1914 maintained that the use of these strategies gave rise to equilibrium (or a 'balance of power') in international affairs and would thereby ensure peace. Liberal historians between the wars argued that it was a defective philosophy that had produced a flawed international system and had led to war. They claimed that the pre-war alliance system and arms build-up associated with it had done nothing to bring about stability but had instead been a source of friction and tension: it had created a climate of suspicion and fear in which Europe had stumbled into war. The implication was that what had failed in 1914 was the system: no one country was to blame.

War by timetable

A variation on the 'shared guilt' theme is the argument that the Great Powers in 1914 found themselves boxed in by the war plans they had made. Perhaps the best-known advocate of this view is the British historian A.J.P. Taylor (1906–1990).

In late July 1914, it is suggested, military considerations began to take priority over everything else. Army chiefs, desperate not to be caught at a disadvantage, took control of the crisis:

- On 29–30 July Russia's generals, knowing that it took six weeks to move the country's widely dispersed forces into position, pressured a hesitant Tsar into ordering mobilisation as a precautionary measure.

- Germany's army commanders demanded the implementation of the Schlieffen Plan.

The Schlieffen Plan

The Schlieffen Plan was the German high command's solution to the problems involved in fighting against France and Russia at the same time. What it wanted to avoid was dividing Germany's forces into two and fighting full-scale campaigns on two fronts against numerically superior opponents. The solution was to take advantage of Russia's inability to mobilise quickly and to defeat France first, before turning to Russia. In order to defeat France within the time available, its array of fortresses on the Franco–German border had to be bypassed. This led to the decision to send Germany's armies into France through Belgium – a decision that involved the violation of Belgian neutrality, a status recognised and agreed by the European Great Powers under the 1839 Treaty of London.

The Schlieffen Plan was Germany's only plan for a war against Russia. A war against Russia therefore inevitably meant a war against France as well. It was in this respect that the Schlieffen Plan limited Germany's options in the July Crisis.

The Schlieffen Plan

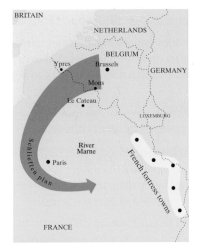

Essential notes

Alfred Von Schlieffen was chief of the general staff (the war planning department) of the German army, 1891–1906. The Schlieffen Plan was produced in 1905. It included arrangements for a logistical operation on a massive scale to switch troops from France to Russia after the anticipated victory in the west: these involved, among other things, the use of 30 000 railway locomotives and 700 000 goods wagons.

Essential notes

Pre-war German claims of 'encirclement' formed the basis of an interpretation of the causes of the First World War put forward by a number of German historical writers between the wars. They argued that 'encirclement' by the Triple *Entente* had forced Germany into fighting a defensive war. It followed that Germany bore no responsibility at all for the outbreak of war in 1914. The 'encirclement' interpretation challenged 'shared guilt', as well as Germany-blaming explanations of the outbreak of war. Few, if any, historians would now subscribe to it.

Examiners' notes

Causation is at the centre of Controversy A. You are therefore likely to be asked questions that present you with one possible cause of the outbreak of war in 1914 and ask you to consider, on the basis of sources and your own knowledge, its importance relative to other causes; for example, 'To what extent was the Schlieffen Plan responsible for the outbreak of war in 1914?'

A useful revision exercise would be to take the core argument of each one of the interpretations outlined here and consider how you would structure an answer to a proposition that it was the main cause of the outbreak of war in 1914.

Overview: Germany's responsibility for the outbreak of war in 1914

Differing interpretations of German responsibility for war in 1914: a summary

Germany-blaming interpretations	'Shared guilt' interpretations	'Encirclement'
Strong version: Germany planned an aggressive war in advance	The war was caused by imperialism	Germany was an innocent victim of aggressive 'encirclement' by the Triple *Entente*
Less extreme version: Germany took the opportunity offered by the July Crisis to fight a preventive war	The war was caused by *Realpolitik*, the alliance system and arms races	
	Inflexible war plans of the Great Powers, especially Germany, were an important cause of war	

Differing interpretations of German responsibility for war: an assessment

The 'strong' Germany-blaming interpretation

- There is evidence suggesting that Germany planned the war in advance (the record of the 1912 Imperial War Council) but it is inconclusive because the record can be read in different ways.

- The 'September Programme' indicates that Germany had well-defined and ambitious war aims but there is no evidence to suggest that it had these aims before 1914: pre-war talk of *Weltpolitik* was vague and often designed for domestic consumption.

The less extreme Germany-blaming interpretation

- Germany's civilian and military leaders were undoubtedly fearful of growing Russian power before 1914.

- This interpretation does not assume that Germany planned a war before 1914, but does suggest that Germany decided to exploit the opportunity offered by the Austro–Serbian dispute in 1914 to begin a war it wanted to fight.

- Some within the German government may have wanted to avoid war in 1914 but were overpowered by others (the military) who did not.

'Shared guilt': imperialism

- Imperialism certainly gave rise to conflict 1870–1914, but the most serious disputes involved Britain, France and Russia – who overcame their differences and combined against Germany.

- Franco–German and Russo–German differences had to do with the situation in Europe and were not 'imperial' in origin.

'Shared guilt': Realpolitik, the alliance system and arms races

- Alliances and arms races were a source of tension before 1914 – the two Morocco crises, for example, originated as attempts to destroy the Anglo–French *entente*.

- The alliance system and arms build-ups had a deterrent effect before 1914 but not in 1914. One explanation for this is that the July Crisis was mismanaged – but a more plausible one is that Germany in 1914 either wanted war or was prepared to risk it.

'Shared guilt': inflexible war plans

Army chiefs certainly used the requirements of their war plans to try to pressure political leaders into making decisions – but it was not inevitable that political leaders would give in to their pressure.

German innocence: 'encirclement'

- Germany's complaints that it was the victim of aggressive encirclement invite the response that the Triple *Entente* was brought into existence not by the aggressive intentions of its members but by belligerent German diplomacy.

- Before 1914 Germany might, with a reasonable chance of success, have attempted to bring about *rapprochements* with both Russia and Britain, but did not do so.

Source 7
(From M.S. Seligmann and R.R. Mclean, *Germany from Reich to Republic, 1871–1918*, Macmillan Press 2000)

We can never establish with certainty when the German decision for war was taken because so much of the documentation which would have helped to establish the answer has been destroyed. However, it seems likely that the decision was taken in response to the assassination of Franz Ferdinand. Berlin's diplomatic actions in the crisis all indicate a preference for war. The military also made no secret of their preference for war.

Germany was the only power which was actively working for a European war in 1914. She was doing so because her leadership, and particularly the military component within it, believed that the international balance of power was shifting inexorably against Germany. This was compounded by their fear of Russia and a perception that Germany was destined to lose the arms race against the *Entente*. Domestic factors were only peripherally involved. The July crisis was regarded as offering Germany a last chance to achieve a European hegemony.

Examiners' notes

Section B questions require you to extract relevant material to develop source-based arguments. If, for example, you were answering the question: 'How far do you agree that German aggression was responsible for the outbreak of a general European war in 1914?', you could use the following points from Source 7:

1. Germany was alone among the Great Powers in the July Crisis in actively seeking to bring about a general European war.
2. Germany's leaders, in particular its army chiefs, were, in 1914, intent on destroying Germany's rivals before they became too powerful to destroy.
3. German policy in 1914 was not designed to overcome internal opposition to the Kaiser's rule but to give Germany a dominant position (hegemony) in Europe.

The Republic's first challenge: the Spartacist Revolt, 1919

Socialist divisions

In late 1918 Germany's socialists were in complete control of the country. Its future was theirs to decide, but they were divided on how to proceed.

The Majority Social Democrats (MSPD) aimed at a democratic republic, while the Spartacus League, a militant faction within the Independent Socialist Party (USPD) that had broken away from the main body of Social Democrats in 1917, favoured a soviet republic. However, most of the USPD shied away from the idea of full Moscow-style communism, but at the same time wanted radical economic, social and political change.

Essential notes

Friedrich Ebert, a former leather worker, was a leading figure in the MSPD and served as the Weimar Republic's first President (1919–25). He was capable and well-intentioned but uncharismatic.

	MSPD	Spartacus League
Leaders	Friedrich Ebert, Philip Schiedemann, Gustav Noske	Karl Liebknecht, Rosa Luxemburg
Political outlook	Moderate democratic socialism	Revolutionary socialism
Aim in 1918	A democratic political system built around a parliament elected by the whole of the German people	A 'dictatorship of the proletariat' in accordance with Marxist theory: a political system based on soviets elected by the working classes alone and the exclusion of middle- and upper-class Germans from the political process
Reason for opposing the other's strategy	Argued that a political system that denied large numbers of citizens' political rights would lack democratic legitimacy	Argued that giving middle- and upper-class Germans the vote would enable them to block Germany's transition to socialism

Essential notes

Karl Liebknecht was an effective orator. The Polish-born Rosa Luxemburg was a formidable writer on socialist theory. During the war, both had served prison sentences for anti-war agitation.

The MSPD forced the issue by calling for the immediate election (by all Germans) of a National Assembly that would be given the responsibility of drawing up a new constitution. This proposal was debated at the All-German Congress of Workers' and Soldiers' Councils in December 1918. As most of the soviets in Germany in late 1918 were under MSPD control, the outcome was a foregone conclusion. The Congress voted 344–98 in favour of National Assembly elections.

After the Congress the USPD left the Provisional Government and the Spartacus League broke away from the USPD to form the German Communist Party (KPD).

The Spartacist uprising, January 1919

Militant socialists, and the KPD in particular, now faced a choice between allowing a democratic Germany to be established without interruption and trying to seize power by force in order to impose socialism on Germany (see diagram opposite).

In January 1919 the Spartacists organised anti-government demonstrations in Berlin. Encouraged by the level of support they received, they launched a bid for power, seizing control of public buildings and declaring that the government had been overthrown.

Ebert's government, recognising the unreliability of the army, had made contingency plans to deal with a KPD *putsch* (an attempted seizure of power by force). Gustav Noske, the Defence Minister, had authorised the formation of privately organised military-style units to help maintain order. These were the so-called Free Corps (*Freikorps*).

In 'Spartacus Week' (5–12 January 1919) the Free Corps crushed KPD forces in Berlin. Liebknecht and Luxemburg were murdered.

With the 'battle for Berlin' won, Noske ordered Free Corps units to move against other centres of revolutionary socialism in Germany:

- Bremen and Hamburg fell to the Free Corps in February 1919.
- A powerful Free Corps presence helped to break a KPD-inspired general strike in the Ruhr (February 1919).
- In May 1919 a 35 000-strong Free Corps army overthrew the KPD-led Bavarian Soviet Republic, which had been proclaimed in Munich in April.

The Free Corps did not, in 1919, eradicate revolutionary socialism as an organised political force in Germany, but they did severely weaken it.

The arguments for and against an armed uprising were balanced

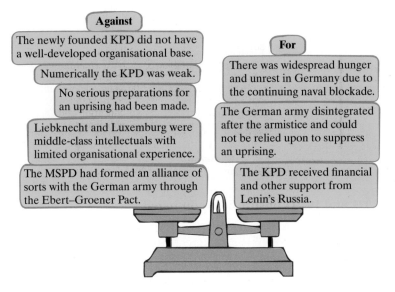

Against

The newly founded KPD did not have a well-developed organisational base.

Numerically the KPD was weak.

No serious preparations for an uprising had been made.

Liebknecht and Luxemburg were middle-class intellectuals with limited organisational experience.

The MSPD had formed an alliance of sorts with the German army through the Ebert–Groener Pact.

For

There was widespread hunger and unrest in Germany due to the continuing naval blockade.

The German army disintegrated after the armistice and could not be relied upon to suppress an uprising.

The KPD received financial and other support from Lenin's Russia.

National Assembly elections, January 1919

The National Assembly elections, held shortly after 'Spartacus Week', resulted in a sweeping victory for those political parties most strongly in favour of a democratic republic – the MSPD, the Democrats (a rebranded version of the Progressive People's Party) and the Centre Party. Between them these three parties won nearly 80 per cent of all votes cast.

The 1919 election result was not as emphatic a victory for democracy as it might appear. What led so many middle-class Germans to vote for the Democrats was not so much democratic zeal as the belief that a Germany ruled by moderates would be generously treated by the Allies at the forthcoming peace conference. Bear in mind, too, that the militant socialist parties took no serious part in the election.

The National Assembly met at Weimar in February 1919 (Berlin was considered too dangerous) and completed its work on the new constitution in June.

Essential notes

Under the Ebert–Groener Pact, army high command undertook to support government efforts to combat 'Bolshevism' in return for a government promise to do what it could to preserve discipline in the army. Groener had succeeded Ludendorff as the army's deputy chief of staff in late 1918.

Examiners' notes

You will be expected to be able to explain the social and political problems faced by the Weimar Republic. You can use the events of January 1919 to show deep political and social divisions in the first months of the Republic.

Essential notes

Free Corps is a plural term: in 1919 there were some 150 separate Free Corps. The largest were over 10 000 strong; the smallest fewer than 500. Total Free Corps strength was around 400 000.

Most originated from regular army units that had remained loyal to their officers, but there were civilian volunteers as well – many of them university students.

The Weimar Constitution

The 1919 Constitution in outline

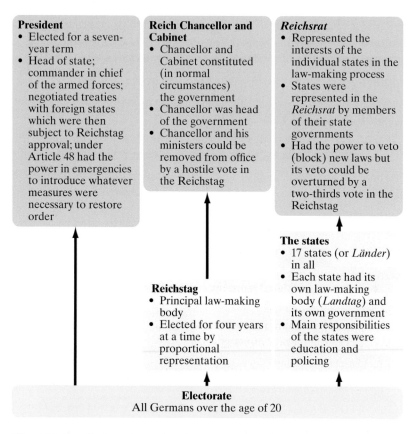

President
- Elected for a seven-year term
- Head of state; commander in chief of the armed forces; negotiated treaties with foreign states which were then subject to Reichstag approval; under Article 48 had the power in emergencies to introduce whatever measures were necessary to restore order

Reich Chancellor and Cabinet
- Chancellor and Cabinet constituted (in normal circumstances) the government
- Chancellor was head of the government
- Chancellor and his ministers could be removed from office by a hostile vote in the Reichstag

Reichsrat
- Represented the interests of the individual states in the law-making process
- States were represented in the *Reichsrat* by members of their state governments
- Had the power to veto (block) new laws but its veto could be overturned by a two-thirds vote in the Reichstag

The states
- 17 states (or *Länder*) in all
- Each state had its own law-making body (*Landtag*) and its own government
- Main responsibilities of the states were education and policing

Reichstag
- Principal law-making body
- Elected for four years at a time by proportional representation

Electorate
All Germans over the age of 20

The 1871 and 1919 Constitutions compared
Differences
Under the 1919 Constitution:

- women had the right to vote in Reichstag elections

- proportional representation was used in elections rather than first past the post

- the head of state was an elected President, not an hereditary monarch

- the Chancellor and his ministers were answerable to the Reichstag on a day-to-day basis and had to resign if they lost the confidence of the Reichstag

- the *Reichsrat* was nothing like as powerful as the Imperial Council had been in the *Kaiserreich* because *Reichsrat* objections to proposed new laws could be overturned by the Reichstag

- the state of Prussia no longer had the power to veto changes to the constitution.

Similarities

There were elements of continuity between the two constitutions:

- Germany remained a federal state
- the principal law-making body was still called the Reichstag (literally, the 'imperial parliament') even though Germany no longer called itself an empire
- the state of Prussia was not broken up into smaller units and remained by far the largest of the German states.

Strengths and weaknesses of the Weimar Constitution

The principal strength of the Weimar Constitution was its ultra-democratic character. Proportional representation and frequent elections were designed to make political institutions responsive to the will of the people. Constitutional guarantees of basic rights (freedom of speech, association and assembly) were designed to encourage popular participation in the political process. So, too, were the arrangements relating to referendums, which could be held in relation to proposed new laws if 10 per cent of voters signed a petition demanding one.

It is sometimes claimed that the main weakness of the 1919 Constitution was the use of proportional representation in Reichstag elections. Two arguments are put forward in support of this view:

- Proportional representation encouraged multi-party politics and by doing so ensured that Weimar governments were weak and unstable coalitions.
- Proportional representation made it easy for extremist parties to win seats in the Reichstag, giving them a credibility they would not otherwise have had.

The first of these arguments is not at all compelling. Multi-party politics in 1920s Germany owed far more to deep-rooted divisions in German society than it did to the electoral system. Remember that the use of 'first past the post' did not prevent multi-party Reichstags in the *Kaiserreich*. The second argument is more persuasive, but its significance should not be overstated: a different electoral system would not have prevented the rise of the Nazis.

Weimar's mixed parliamentary–presidential arrangement was a bigger source of difficulty than proportional representation. The intention of the 1919 Constitution-makers was that Germany should function as a parliamentary democracy on British lines. But they did not establish a British-style, purely ceremonial head of state. Instead they gave the President substantial political power, in particular the ability under Article 48 to rule by decree in an emergency. This arrangement was open to abuse and was abused after 1930.

Like most constitutions, the Weimar Constitution had its defects, but it was not so badly flawed as to be unworkable.

Essential notes

Systems of proportional representation try to achieve a close fit between the share of the national vote a party wins in an election and the share of the seats it receives in parliament. Under proportional representation, a party winning 40 per cent of the votes will receive 40 per cent of the seats.

In 'first past the post' elections the party winning the largest number of votes in each constituency wins the seat. 'First past the post' does not produce a 'proportional' result overall: it over-rewards parties whose support is concentrated in particular localities and under-rewards parties whose support is more thinly spread.

Essential notes

Rule by decree involves an individual or small group of people introducing new laws without having to secure the approval of an elected law-making body.

Parties and governments in the 1920s

Political parties

The only political party to emerge from the war completely unchanged was the Centre Party. However, the changes that took place as a result of the war were largely cosmetic: the middle-class parties renamed themselves and the two conservative parties, allies before 1914, merged. The most significant change in the party system brought about by the war was the split in the working-class camp, which left the SPD and KPD vying with each other for working-class support.

Right ◄————————————————————————————————► Left

	Nationalist Party (DNVP)	People's Party (DVP)	Centre Party	Democratic Party (DDP)	Social Democrats (SPD)	Independent Socialists (USPD)	Communists (KPD)
Origins	A merger of the German Conservative Party and the Free Conservatives	A rebranded version of the National Liberal Party	Thought of renaming itself the Christian People's Party in 1918, but decided against it	Rebranded version of the Progressive People's Party	The pre-war SPD minus its militant left wing	Founded 1917 as a breakaway party from the mainstream SPD; disbanded 1922	Founded 1919 as a breakaway party from the USPD
Leading figures	Count von Westarp Alfred Hugenberg	Gustav Stresemann	Matthias Erzberger	Walter Rathenau	Freidrich Ebert Philip Scheidemann Gustav Noske	Hugo Haase	Karl Liebknecht Rosa Luxemburg Ernst Thälmann
Electoral support	Junkers; industrial tycoons; farmers; some of the middle class	Upper-middle classes; business community	Catholics of all social classes	Intellectuals; professional classes	Working classes, especially skilled workers; some lower-middle class	Working classes	Working classes, especially unskilled workers
Best election result 1919–30	21% (1924)	14% (1920)	20% (1919)	19% (1919)	38% (1919)	17% (1920)	13% (1930)
Worst election result 1919–30	7% (1930)	5% (1930)	15% (1930)	4% (1930)	21% (1920)	8% (1919)	2% (1920)

☐ Anti-Republic ☐ Initially anti-Republic ☐ Pro-Republic

Governments

In the 1920s, as before 1914, Germany not only had a multi-party system but a multi-party system of a distinctive kind. Some parties were more consistently successful in electoral terms than others, but there was no clear-cut distinction between major and minor parties. No party ever came close to winning a 50 per cent share of the vote in the Reichstag elections of the 1920s: the best single result was the 38 per cent achieved by the SPD in 1919. On the other hand, there were six parties (seven if the Nazi result in 1930 is included) that won 10 per cent or more of the vote in at least one election between 1919 and 1930.

In these circumstances there was no possibility of either a single-party or two-party coalition government. Weimar's distinctive multi-party system meant that coalition governments with majority support in the Reichstag could only be formed if three or four parties were willing to participate.

The process of coalition formation was complicated by the refusal of the anti-Republican parties to take part in the work of government. The KPD never joined coalitions and the DNVP did so only briefly under the relatively moderate leadership of Count von Westarp in the mid-1920s. Remember, too, that the SPD was uneasy about governing in partnership with non-socialists. It entered coalitions at the beginning and end of the 1920s but, in Weimar's middle years of the Republic, mostly left the work of government in the hands of the middle-class parties.

Three- or four-party coalitions are more likely to fall apart than single-party governments.

In the years 1919–30, 16 different coalition governments held office.

The four types of coalition

Coalition type	Parties involved	Number formed, 1919–30
The 'Weimar' coalition	SPD-DDP-Centre	5
The 'middle-class' coalition	DDP-Centre-DVP	6
The 'right-wing' coalition	Centre-DVP-DNVP	2
The 'grand coalition'	SPD-DDP-Centre-DVP	3

Government in Weimar Germany was not as chaotic and unstable as the headline figure of 16 different ministries in 11 years might suggest. There was continuity as well as change: the Centre Party sat in all 16 Weimar governments, the DDP in 14 out of 16 and the DVP in 11 out of 16.

Essential notes

A coalition government is one made up of two or more political parties.

Examiners' notes

You would not be expected to remember precise figures relating to the electoral performance of the main political parties, but you should have an understanding of the sections of society from which the parties drew their support and of the main trends in changing support in the 1920s and early 1930s. The Nazis, excluded from the table below, are considered in the next chapter.

Essential notes

The 'Weimar' coalition was so called because it consisted of those parties that most strongly favoured a democratic Republic on principle. Stresemann's DVP was not instinctively republican (it was monarchist) but came to believe there was no feasible alternative to the Republic.

Crises and survival, 1919–24

The events of 1918–19 led to dramatic political change in Germany. It would be a mistake, however, to think that they transformed Germany completely. Alongside the changes that took place there were elements of continuity. Senior civil servants, police chiefs and judges who had held office in Imperial Germany were allowed to remain in their posts, with the result that many key positions in German public life in the 1920s were occupied by people who were enemies of democracy. Nor did the events of 1918–19 lead to significant changes in the distribution of wealth in Germany. Banks and industries remained under private ownership, and the rich retained their wealth.

The principal threat to the survival of the Weimar Republic in the early 1920s came from the extreme right.

Who were the anti-Republican right?

The anti-Republican right's core supporters in the early 1920s came from the conservative elites, the displaced ruling class of the *Kaiserreich* – the *Junkers*, army officers and industrial tycoons.

The main political party of the anti-Republican right was the Nationalist Party (DNVP). It was not a mass party: its average share of the vote in the Reichstag elections of the 1920s was around 10 per cent.

The DNVP's leaders made little effort to broaden its appeal because – like most others on the anti-Republican right – they envisaged regaining power not via the ballot box but through a *putsch*. The anti-Republican right was well placed to seize power by force:

- It had the support of much of the officer corps of the German army.

- It was backed by a large number of right-wing paramilitary organisations formed in the early 1920s. The biggest of them was the *Stahlhelm* ('Steel Helmets'), nominally a war veterans' association but in practice closely linked with the DNVP.

- It had the capacity to influence public opinion through the media outlets at its disposal. A key figure here was the film and newspaper tycoon Alfred Hugenberg.

Far right attitudes to the Republic

Members of Germany's conservative elites were irreconcilably opposed to the Republic for three main reasons:

1. They resented the loss of the power and status they had enjoyed before 1918 and which they regarded as theirs by right.

2. They saw the Weimar Republic as the handiwork of those they regarded as the worst elements in German society (socialists, Catholics and Jews), dismissing it contemptuously as a *Sozi-republik* (Social Democratic Republic) and a *Judenrepublik* (Jewish Republic).

3. They convinced themselves that Weimar politicians were to blame for Germany's defeat in 1918 and for the *Schmachfrieden* ('shameful peace') of 1919.

Essential notes

Alfred Hugenberg (1865–1951) was a media tycoon. He owned local and national newspapers, Germany's biggest press agency and a major film studio. He was also a prominent member of the DNVP, becoming its leader in 1928.

Essential notes

Anti-Republican right-wingers maintained that Weimar politicians had, in November 1918, agreed to an armistice even though the German army had been capable of fighting on. Consequently, they described the Weimar politicians as 'November Criminals' who had stabbed the army in the back. Though false, the *Dolchstosslegende* (stab in the back myth) was widely believed in 1920s Germany.

The Treaty of Versailles, 1919

Having led Germany to defeat in 1918, the conservative elites found themselves discredited and politically marginalised. But they recovered extraordinarily quickly. Key to the revival of their political fortunes was the Treaty of Versailles and the reparations issue that arose out of it. An awareness of the terms of the Treaty and of the reasons why it caused outrage in Germany is therefore important.

Treaty of Versailles: summary of terms

Territorial losses in Europe

- Losses without a plebiscite: Alsace-Lorraine (to France); Eupen and Malmédy (to Belgium); Posen and West Prussia (to Poland, creating the 'Polish Corridor'); the city of Danzig (became a free city under League of Nations control); Memel (occupied by France but ceded to Lithuania, 1923).

- Losses following a plebiscite: North Schleswig (to Denmark); Upper Silesia (to Poland).

- The Rhineland became a demilitarised zone, with the west (or left) bank region occupied by Allied forces for 15 years.

- The Saar was placed under League of Nations control for 15 years during which time its coal mines were to be under French administration: after 15 years a plebiscite was to be held to determine its future.

Military clauses

- Army: restricted to 100 000 men; no conscription (to prevent the rapid build-up of a reservoir of trained manpower); no tanks or heavy artillery; no general staff.

- Navy: restricted to 15 000 men; no submarines; German fleet limited to 6 battleships of less than 10 000 tons, 6 cruisers and 12 destroyers; existing battle fleet to be surrendered to the British.

- Air force: none permitted.

Colonial losses

- All German colonies in Africa and the Pacific were forfeited and became League of Nations mandates.

Reparations

- Article 231 of the Treaty (the 'war guilt' clause) held Germany responsible for all loss and damage suffered by the Allies during the war and provided the basis for reparations.

- The total sum due was not fixed in 1919 but was to be decided by an Inter-Allied Reparations Commission (which reported in 1921 and fixed Germany's liability at £6600 million or 132 billion marks).

Essential notes

A plebiscite is a vote that allows all of the qualified voters of a country or region to express their support for, or opposition to, a proposed political change.

☞ Continued on the next four pages

Territorial settlement in Europe

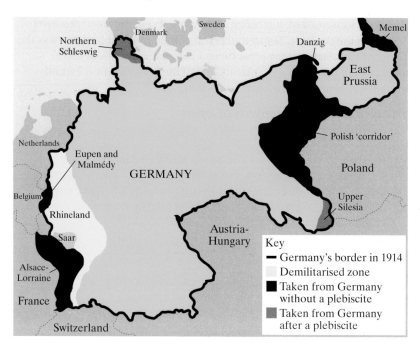

German hostility to the Versailles Treaty

Germans regarded the Treaty as an outrage for a variety of reasons, but three stand out.

The Diktat

Germans expected to negotiate a peace agreement with the Allies but a settlement was imposed on them without talks. Germans further expected that the peace settlement would be based on Woodrow Wilson's January 1918 proposals for a compromise peace – the Fourteen Points – but they were disregarded.

The 'Polish Corridor'

The arrangements designed to give the new state of Poland access to the sea aroused deep resentment because one million Germans were put under Polish rule without being given any say in the matter – a proceeding, said Germans, inconsistent with the Allied commitment to the principle of national self-determination. In addition, East Prussia was cut off from the rest of Germany.

War guilt and reparations

Germans dismissed the 'war guilt' clause as the 'war guilt lie' and, as a result, viewed Allied reparation demands as illegitimate. The sums demanded in reparations were also felt to be unpayable. It was widely assumed that the Allies' aim was simply to wreck the German economy.

Essential notes

In fact, not all of these people were in the Polish corridor. Many were in Posen, where urban areas were sometimes German while the countryside was Polish.

How did the peace settlement help the far right to make a political comeback in Germany?

- Many Germans shared the far right's view that Germany should refuse to sign the Versailles Treaty and condemned Republican leaders for agreeing to it. In this way the Treaty simultaneously discredited Republicans and boosted the anti-Republican right.

- The language of defiant nationalism went down well in post-Versailles Germany – and the far right spoke it far more naturally and plausibly than moderates and progressives.

- When the anti-Republican right claimed that the German army had not been defeated but stabbed in the back they were saying what many people wanted to hear.

- The Treaty undermined the Republic by leaving political moderates – who had argued that the Allies would behave leniently towards a democratic Germany – looking naive.

The Kapp *Putsch*, 1920

The military clauses of the Versailles Treaty triggered the first attempt by the far right to overthrow the Republic by force.

Noske had promised the Free Corps that they would in due course be incorporated into the regular army. The imposition of a limit of 100 000 on the size of the German army left him unable to fulfil his promise. Instead he found himself having to disband most of the Free Corps.

In 1920 Herman Ehrhardt, commander of a Free Corps notorious for its brutality, responded to an order to disband by planning to topple the government that had issued it. He drew into his plans Wolfgang Kapp, a minor far-right politician, and Walther von Luttwitz, a serving general in the German army. Ehrhardt's forces were able briefly to occupy Berlin because the army refused to move against them. However, Ehrhardt, Kapp and Luttwitz failed to win the active support of others on the anti-Republican right and their *putsch* attempt petered out. An SPD-led general strike in defence of the Republic also contributed to its failure.

Organisational Consul, 1920–2

After the failure of his frontal assault on the Republic in 1920, Ehrhardt – on the run from the authorities – turned to political assassination as a means of destabilising it. He formed a murder gang, Organisation Consul, which proceeded to carry out a series of attacks on prominent Republicans. Organisation Consul was responsible for the deaths of Matthias Erzberger (1921), the Centre Party leader who negotiated the November 1918 Armistice, and Walter Rathenau (1922), Germany's (Jewish) Foreign Minister. An attempt on the life of Philip Scheidemann (1922) failed. The murder of Rathenau led to a security crackdown that put Organisation Consul out of business.

Essential notes

When the government called upon the German army to put down the Kapp *Putsch*, its commander, Hans von Seeckt, famously replied 'troops do not fire on troops'.

Continued on the next two pages

Essential notes

Inflation can be defined as a state of affairs in which prices are steadily rising and the value of money is steadily falling. The term 'hyperinflation' is used to describe a situation in which prices are rising so rapidly that confidence in money as a medium of exchange collapses.

The crisis of 1923

Inflation to hyperinflation

Germany had a serious inflation problem before 1923:

- It had paid for the war not by increasing taxes but by borrowing and printing money. This led to inflation.

- The post-war reparations settlement dented international confidence in Germany's currency (the mark). The value of the mark in relation to other currencies fell, which meant that the cost of Germany's imports rose, pushing up the cost of living.

In 1923 France, in line with its policy of strict enforcement of the Versailles Treaty, sent troops into the Ruhr when Germany failed to make a reparations payment on schedule. Germany, shorn of its military strength by the Treaty, opted for a policy of passive resistance. This involved calling on the Ruhr's industrial workers to go out on strike and compensating them for their lost wages. Passive resistance led to a ballooning deficit in Germany's public finances (expenditure went up as a result of payments to the Ruhr strikers and tax receipts fell because the Ruhr was at a standstill). The government financed the budget deficit by printing paper money. This policy destroyed what was left of the confidence in the mark and led to its total collapse.

Economic impact of hyperinflation

Winners and losers

Winners	Temporary losers	Permanent losers
People who owed money and who were able to pay off their debts in worthless currency – for example, businessmen who had borrowed money to invest and landowners who had mortgaged their estates.	People who neither owed money nor had substantial savings but whose wages failed to keep pace with inflation in the course of 1923.	People who had saved money and saw the value of their savings wiped out. Those who lost out in this way did not receive compensation.
Adroit speculators such as the industrial tycoon Hugo Stinnes were able to make huge fortunes.	People in this category found it difficult to buy food, fuel and other necessities in late 1923, but they recovered quickly when the currency was stabilised.	Examples include: those with money in bank accounts, pensioners, those who had invested in war bonds in the 1914–18 war.
In the main, the winners came from the wealthier sections of German society.	Most people in this category were working class.	Most people in this category were middle class.

Overall, though, the biggest winner was the government, whose war debts disappeared. Consequently, the biggest losers were members of the middle and upper classes, who subscribed to war loans.

Social and political unrest

In early 1923 trades unions were able to negotiate wage increases that allowed wages to keep up with rising prices. In mid-1923, however, prices surged ahead of wages, leaving working-class families struggling to buy food. As a result, serious unrest broke out in the poorer districts of Germany's major cities in the shape of strikes, hunger riots and looting. These were circumstances the KPD could turn to its advantage: in 1923 it made plans to seize control of Saxony before turning its attention to the rest of the country.

Circumstances in late 1923 were also conducive to a right-wing *putsch* attempt:

- The French occupation of the Ruhr gave rise to a mood of intense nationalism in Germany.

- Fears of a communist *putsch* were widespread among the middle and upper classes.

- The abandonment of passive resistance (September 1923), a decision forced on the government by the breakdown of law and order, enabled the anti-Republican right to claim that the Republic had capitulated to the French.

Prominent supporters of the anti-Republican right involved at this point in discussions about a *putsch* attempt included Hugenberg, von Seeckt, Ludendorff and Stinnes. Their plans involved using Bavaria, where the far right state government was headed by Gustav von Kahr, as a launching pad for a march on Berlin.

In the event, the far right conspiracy unravelled. The leading conspirators dithered. In Munich Ludendorff and Hitler's Nazi paramilitaries, the SA, tried to force the issue by taking to the streets. They were fired upon by police units loyal to von Kahr: 14 were killed.

Why was the Republic able to survive the threats to its existence in the early 1920s?

The principal weakness of the far left was that it lacked popular support: only a minority of the German working class sided with the KPD.

The anti-Republican right also lacked widespread popular support but its most important weakness was internal disunity. At no point during 1919–23 did it attack the Republic in a concerted fashion, bringing all of the resources available to it into play. Internal divisions were a significant factor in the failure of both the 1920 and 1923 *putsch* attempts.

The Republic did not owe its survival solely to its enemies' weaknesses. There was in Germany a sizeable body of opinion, with the SPD at its core, which was strongly committed to the democratic experiment. Furthermore, the Republic's supporters were resolute in its defence. Noske unleashed the Free Corps on the far left in 1919; SPD trades unionists contributed to the defeat of the Kapp *Putsch* in 1920 by joining a general strike; and in 1922 half a million supporters of the Republic came out on to the streets of Berlin in protest against the murder of Rathenau by the Organisation Consul.

Essential notes

Germany's trades unions were more powerful in the 1920s than they had been before 1914. Union membership increased sharply in the early 1920s. The unions were also ready to flex their muscles: the number of working days lost through strike action in the 1920s was markedly higher than in the years 1900–14.

Essential notes

The events in Munich on 8–9 November 1923, involving Hitler and Ludendorff, became known as the Munich *Putsch* or the Beer Hall *Putsch*. Note that both sets of participants in the clash that took place were adherents of the anti-Republican right. No forces loyal to the Republic were involved.

Essential notes

Gustav Stresemann (1878–1929) was leader of the DVP and a pragmatic conservative. Early in his political career he was an extreme right-winger: in the wartime Reichstag he advocated an all-out war policy. After the war he remained a monarchist, voting against the draft constitution in the 1919 National Assembly and failing to come out against the Kapp *Putsch* in 1920. The murder of Rathenau (1922) helped to convince him that there was no workable alternative to the Republic, and it was on this basis he entered government in 1923. Stresemann was what was called a *Vernunftrepublikaner* ('a republican by circumstances').

Stresemann and stabilisation, 1923–9

Stresemann as Chancellor, August–November 1923

Stresemann came into office as head of a four-party 'grand coalition' when hyperinflation was at its worst. In his three months as Chancellor he did his country three major services:

- He called off passive resistance (September 1923). With the German economy paralysed, barter replacing the use of paper money and law and order breaking down, it had become an unsustainable policy. The decision to abandon passive resistance nevertheless required political courage: Stresemann knew that it would be used by the far right as the pretext for an attack on the Republic. Civil war appeared to be a distinct possibility.

- He oversaw the introduction of a new currency to replace the worthless mark. The new currency (known first as the *Rentenmark* and then as the *Reichsmark)* was issued in strictly limited quantities so that it would retain its value. One trillion old marks were exchangeable for one *Rentenmark*. The establishment of a stable currency paved the way for the return of normal economic life: people no longer had to resort to barter.

- He fended off threats to the Republic's survival from the extreme left and the extreme right. He defeated the communist threat by ordering the army into Saxony and overcame the extreme right by waiting until it self-destructed in the Beer Hall *Putsch*.

Stresemann's policies led to friction inside his coalition. The SPD, angered by the contrast between aggressive interventionism in Saxony and non-interventionism in Bavaria, left the government. Stresemann was forced to resign the Chancellorship.

Stresemann as Foreign Minister, 1923–9

'Fulfilment'

German opinion was united in its hatred of the Versailles *Diktat* but divided on the issue of how to go about overturning it. The anti-Republican right called for a policy of non-cooperation – refusing to pay reparations, ignoring the Treaty's military clauses and daring the Allies to do their worst. Moderates advocated a more subtle and realistic approach – 'fulfilment policy'. 'Fulfilment' involved attempting to improve relations with the Allies by complying with the terms of the Versailles Treaty in the hope that they would, once persuaded of Germany's good intentions, be willing to modify or revise it.

Rathenau and Wirth pioneered the policy of 'fulfilment' in the early 1920s but Stresemann was its most effective practitioner. The anti-Republican right saw 'fulfilment' as an outrage, arguing that by agreeing to pay reparations Germany was in effect accepting the 'war guilt lie'.

Stresemann's foreign policy and its domestic significance

Achievement	What was involved?	Domestic significance
Dawes Plan, 1924	A stop-gap reparations agreement between Germany and the Allies. Germany agreed to resume payments (suspended when the Ruhr was occupied in early 1923) in return for a reduction in the amount payable each year. Germany received a sizeable loan ($200 million) from the USA to help it restart reparations payments.	Accepted by political moderates because it paved the way for French withdrawal from the Ruhr. Attacked by the anti-Republican right on the grounds that Germany was being 'enslaved' – because the Dawes Plan gave the Allies supervisory powers over Germany's national bank to ensure that payments were made.
Locarno Pact, 1925, and entry into League of Nations, 1926	At Locarno, France and Germany agreed not to change by force the border between the two countries laid down by the Treaty of Versailles. Germany became a member of the League as a permanent member of its prestigious Council (along with Britain, France, Italy and Japan).	Again divisive. Political moderates welcomed the Locarno Pact and entry into the League because they ended Germany's isolation within the international community. The anti-Republican right, by contrast, argued that these arrangements implied acceptance of Versailles and that Locarno 'betrayed the nation' by effectively abandoning German claims to Alsace-Lorraine.
Young Plan, 1929	An agreement between Germany and the Allies that replaced the 1924 Dawes Plan and was intended to be a final settlement of the reparations issue. Germany's total reparations liability was reduced from the £6600 million to £1850 million.	Stresemann was able to declare that Germany was now free of all foreign occupying forces – seen by moderates as a huge achievement. The anti-Republican right claimed that the Young Plan schedule of 58 annual repayments starting in 1930 would 'enslave' Germany until 1988.

Stresemann's foreign policy and its domestic impact

The significance of Stresemann's foreign policy

Stresemann's foreign policy opened the way to the return of prosperity at home. Rid of hyperinflation and rehabilitated within the international community, Germany became highly attractive to foreign investors. Foreign investment kick-started German economic growth in the later 1920s. Republicans recognised the importance of Stresemann's contribution to the return of economic normalcy: when he died the SPD newspaper *Vorwärts* claimed that he had led Germany 'from devastation to recovery'.

On the other hand, Stresemann's foreign policy was deeply unpopular with those on the anti-Republican right. They hurled the 'enslavement' charge at Stresemann again and again. In 1929 the DNVP (with Nazi backing) forced a referendum on a proposed law that, had it been passed by the Reichstag, would have branded Stresemann a national traitor.

Examiners' notes

When assessing the relative importance of Stresemann's contribution to the recovery of the later 1920s, remember that he did not bring about recovery single-handedly. Rathenau originated the 'fulfilment policy'; Ebert used his emergency powers as President to help keep the Republic afloat in 1923; Schacht (banker) and Luther (Finance Minister) made detailed preparations for the launch of the *Rentenmark*; Stresemann's coalition partners gave him room for manoeuvre; Britain and France adopted accommodating policies; the USA was heavily involved in the making of the Dawes and Young Plans.

Essential notes

The Bauhaus was an institute for the study of art and design dedicated to breaking down barriers between the pure and applied arts. Some of Germany's leading *avant-garde* artists were on its staff. It was shut down by the Nazis in 1933.

Weimar culture and society

The arts

The Weimar era was one of exceptional cultural vibrancy. In the arts a dazzling array of talent was at work.

Famous names of the Weimar era

Literature	Visual arts	Music
Bertolt Brecht	Otto Dix	**Composers:**
Alfred Döblin	Max Ernst	Paul Hindemith
Hans Fallada	George Grosz	Arnold Schoenberg
Thomas Mann	John Heartfield	Kurt Weill
Erich Maria Remarque	Paul Klee	
	Käthe Kollwitz	**Conductors:**
	Wassily Kandinsky	Wilhelm Furtwängler
		Otto Klemperer

Popular culture

1920s Germany saw a boom in popular entertainment as well as extraordinary creativity in the arts.

In the 1920s Germany was home to Europe's most innovative and successful film-makers. The biggest production company was Ufa (*Universum Film AG*), which had its studio at Babelsberg outside Berlin. Leading figures in the film industry included the actors Marlene Dietrich and Peter Lorre and the directors Fritz Lang, G.W. Pabst and Josef von Sternberg. The cinema was hugely popular in Germany in the 1920s: in 1926, 332 million cinema tickets were sold.

Berlin was the entertainment capital of Europe in the 1920s. After the abolition of censorship in 1919 night clubs, revues and cabaret venues sprang up by the score. They offered a blend of song, dance, stand-up comedy and political satire. Some were high-brow, many seedy, but they played an important role in defining what is now termed 'Weimar culture'.

The highest-profile spectator sports in 1920s Germany were raw, confrontational ones such as boxing and six-day bicycle racing.

Culture wars

Inside Germany Weimar culture was controversial and divisive. Cultural issues set modernists against traditionalists, Berlin against the provinces and the political left against the political right.

Weimar writers, artists and composers were for the most part experimental and *avant-garde*. Traditionalists often found their work bewildering and upsetting. To those with a preference for representational painting, the extreme abstract works of Weimar painters such as Klee and Kandinsky were puzzling; to those with a liking for harmony and melody in music, the jazz-influenced compositions of Weill and Hindemith were jarring; and to those brought up to admire elaborately decorated 19th-century buildings, the simple, clean lines of Bauhaus architecture were disconcerting.

Weimar culture was Berlin-centred. Outside Berlin, cultural life was more conventional and less racy than it was in the capital. In 1920s Frankfurt, for example, there were only three nightclubs. Many Germans living in the provinces in the Weimar era viewed Berlin as a decadent, even wicked, place.

Many of the leading artists and writers in the Weimar era had strong left-wing sympathies. George Grosz, John Heartfield and Bertolt Brecht, for example, were active members of the Communist Party. In their works they attacked Germany's political right as brutal, corrupt and oppressive. Conservatives replied in kind. A common charge was that left-wing writers and artists showed contempt for traditional German values and, by doing so, were corrupting the young. In support of their claim conservatives pointed to the sharp rise in rates of crime, divorce and abortion in 1920s Germany.

Social tensions

Social tensions increased in Germany in the later 1920s, largely as a result of the anxieties and resentment felt within the middle classes. Many middle-class Germans in the late 1920s were embittered by what they saw as unfair treatment:

- One reason for this sense of injustice was hyperinflation, which had wiped away the savings of many middle-class households. No compensation for these losses was forthcoming. Among those who felt especially let down were those middle-class Germans who had patriotically invested in war bonds back in 1914 and who had been left with nothing as a result of hyperinflation.

- The return to prosperity in the later 1920s did little to improve the mood within the middle classes. The feeling within the middle class was that the benefits of increased prosperity went disproportionately to the working classes. Trades unions succeeded in winning significant increases in real wages for their members, narrowing the gap between middle- and working-class incomes. The working classes benefited, too, from increased social welfare spending. The 1927 Unemployment Insurance Act offered support to workers who had lost their jobs, in the form of six months' unemployment benefit. Middle-class Germans complained that their taxes were being misspent.

- Many self-employed middle-class Germans struggled economically in the later 1920s: the livelihoods of skilled craftsmen were threatened by cheap mass-produced goods, while shopkeepers were faced with competition from fast-growing networks of department stores.

Essential notes

A flashpoint in Weimar's culture wars was the 'Law for the Protection of Youth against Trash and Filth' of 1926. This was a successful attempt by the political right and the churches to outlaw displays and exhibitions which could corrupt the young. The Law was opposed by communists, Social Democrats and democrats who saw it as a restriction on freedom of expression.

Essential notes

Stresemann reflected on the plight of German middle classes when he accepted the Nobel Peace Prize in 1927.

'The intellectual and professional middle class, which traditionally upheld the idea of service to the state, paid for its total devotion to the state during the war with the total loss of its own wealth, and with its consequent reduction to the level of the working class. All that has taken place in Germany since the war must be looked at in the light of the mood of this completely uprooted class. Theirs was an economic uprooting. But there was a mental and political uprooting, as well.'

The later 1920s: 'golden years' of the Weimar Republic?

Economic 'golden years'?

The later 1920s are sometimes described as the 'golden years' of the Weimar Republic. It is too generous a verdict. The post-1923 economic recovery did not rest on secure foundations. In the political sphere the extremist threat appeared to recede but appearances were deceptive.

> **Source 1**
> (Gustav Stresemann, 1924)
>
> The German economy is doing well only on the surface. Germany is in fact dancing on a volcano. If the short-term loans are called in by America, most of our economy will collapse.

The economy in the later 1920s: positives and negatives

Positives	Negatives
With the currency stabilised and the return of a measure of normality, Germany in the late 1920s became a magnet for foreign investors, especially from the USA.	Prosperity was heavily dependent on foreign investment, much of which took the form of loans and credits that could be withdrawn at short notice. The Dawes and Young Plans linked Germany's fortunes closely to those of the USA – with damaging consequences after the 1919 Wall Street Crash.
German businessmen took advantage of low interest rates and easy credit to upgrade their plants and machinery.	
A process of mergers and takeovers saw the emergence of vast industrial combines (such as the chemicals giant IG Farben) which benefited from economies of scale.	The agricultural sector of the economy did not share in the general prosperity. World food prices were low in the later 1920s and farmers' incomes suffered as a result. Unable to make ends meet, farmers went heavily into debt and bitterly resented the failure of the Republic to do more to help them.
Industrial output increased sharply in the later 1920s.	
German exports increased by 50 per cent between 1925 and 1929.	
There were significant increases in workers' real wages in the later 1920s: standards of living were higher in 1929 than they had been on the eve of war in 1914.	Unemployment was higher than might have been expected in a period of economic recovery: the use of mass production techniques enabled employers to cut their workforce.
Housing conditions improved dramatically as local authorities took advantage of cheap loans to embark on massive house-building schemes.	Governments lived beyond their means, financing budget deficit by borrowing. High levels of borrowing could not be sustained indefinitely.

Essential notes

When Hindenburg agreed to run for the Presidency in 1925 (entering in the second ballot – the first produced no clear winner) he made no secret of his anti-Republican sympathies. He remained, for example, an honorary member of the extreme right-wing *Stahlhelm*. Anti-Republican right-wingers hoped and expected that his election would lead to a more authoritarian form of government. In the short term they were disappointed. Between 1925 and 1930 Hindenburg was not a disruptive influence. He supported Stresemann's foreign policy, confining himself to minor anti-Republican gestures (such as insisting in 1926 that the black-white-red flag of Germany's merchant navy – the colours of Imperial Germany – be flown outside German embassies alongside the Republic's black-red-gold flag).

The later 1920s: political stability?

Two developments suggested that the Republic's survival prospects may have been improving in the later 1920s:

- There were no major *putsch* attempts in this period.

- The anti-Republican right suffered heavy losses in the Reichstag elections of 1928. In December 1924, with memories of the French occupation of the Ruhr fresh in voters' minds, the Nationalists won 21 per cent of the vote: in 1928 this figure slumped to 14 per cent.

On the other hand, there was evidence of continuing and perhaps worsening difficulties:

- The problem of short-lived three- or four-party coalition governments remained.

- When Ebert died in 1925 he was succeeded as President by Hindenburg, a sworn enemy of parliamentary democracy.

- Street violence involving paramilitary forces became an increasingly serious problem. The worst clashes were between the Nazi SA, given the task of conquering the streets by Hitler in 1925, and the communist *Roter Frontkämpferbund* (Red Front or Red Front Fighters' League), founded 1924. Also involved on occasion were the SPD-linked *Reichsbanner* and the anti-Republican *Stahlhelm*.

Numbers killed in political violence in Germany, 1924–9

Nazis	29
Communists	92
Stahlhelm	26
Reichsbanner	18
Total	162

- In the late 1920s the middle classes were, for a number of reasons, becoming increasingly alienated from the Republic:

1. They blamed the Republic for their financial losses in 1923.

2. They complained about living in a *Gewerkschaftstaat* or 'trades union state' – that is, one in which the workers always received favourable treatment.

3. They believed that the Republic was somehow responsible for social trends many of them found unwelcome – the 'New Woman', rising crime rates, juvenile delinquency, sexual permissiveness and the commercialisation of leisure. The term 'cultural pessimism' is used to describe the outlook mind-set of those who were unsettled by these trends.

4. They were angered by scandals involving prominent supporters of the Republic – notably the Barmat scandal (1924–5) in which senior SPD figures received soft loans from Barmat Enterprises (a company run by four Polish Jewish brothers who had emigrated to Germany before 1914) in return for political favours.

Examiners' notes

The Specification requires you to be able to analyse the role of Hindenburg in German politics in the 1920s and early 1930s. Make sure you bring together the information you will find about Hindenburg in different chapters of this book. Hindenburg was significant in the revolution of 1918 (see pages 4–19) and influential in the 1920s as you can see on these pages. He also played an important part in the events leading to the end of the Weimar Republic in the early 1930s (see pages 56–67).

Essential notes

The phrase 'New Woman' was used in 1920s Germany to describe women who turned their backs on traditional domestic roles and who lived independent, career-oriented, sexually emancipated lives. Conservatives saw the 'New Woman' as selfish, materialistic and immoral. There were, in practice, nothing like as many 'New Women' in 1920s Germany as conservative writers suggested.

Essential notes

A soft loan is one that is offered at a rate of interest below the going rate.

Origins of the NSDAP to 1928

Adolf Hitler, 1889–1945

- He was by birth a citizen of the Austrian Empire: he took German citizenship only in 1932.

- His unsuccessful school career and failure to secure a place in higher education left him with a lasting contempt for intellectuals.

- His failure to hold down a regular job in Vienna before 1914 meant that he never acquired the habit of disciplined and systematic work.

- Hitler became an anti-Semite in pre-war Vienna but his anti-Semitism was intensified by Germany's defeat in 1918: he believed Jews were foremost among those who had 'stabbed the German army in the back'.

Origins of the NSDAP

The precursor of the NSDAP was Anton Drexler's German Workers' Party (DAP). In 1919 Hitler infiltrated it while working as a V-Man (a low-level undercover agent) for the German army. He became active in its affairs and discovered that he had a gift for public speaking. In 1920 he left the army to devote himself to the DAP on a full-time basis, soon becoming its chairman.

In the early 1920s Hitler set out to transform what was not much more than a political debating society into a serious political force:

- A policy statement, the Twenty-Five Point Programme, was published in 1920.

- The party changed its name to the NSDAP (National Socialist German Workers' Party).

- A party newspaper, the *Volkischer Beobachter* ('People's Observer'), was launched in 1920.

- A network of party branches, most of them in Bavaria, was established and a programme of public meetings was organised.

- A paramilitary organisation, the SA ('storm troop') was formed in 1921.

The NSDAP in the later 1920s

After the fiasco of the Beer Hall *Putsch* (1923), Hitler was sentenced to five years' imprisonment for treason. The NSDAP was outlawed. On his early release from prison (1925) he set about relaunching it.

Hitler's first priority was to unify the party under his control. While he was in prison, bickering had broken out between Munich-based Hitler loyalists and the strongly anti-capitalist north German wing of the party, headed by Gregor Strasser. At the Bamberg Conference (1926), Hitler reasserted his authority, making it clear there would be no revision of party policy along anti-capitalist lines.

In the later 1920s Hitler tightened his grip over the NSDAP by imposing the *Führerprinzip* ('leadership principle') on it.

The *putsch* was abandoned as a means of gaining power. In its place a strategy of 'legality' was adopted. 'Legality' involved contesting elections

Essential notes

The word 'Nazi' originated as a slang term used by the NSDAP's opponents: it was a shortened version of the party's full name. NSDAP members called themselves National Socialists, not Nazis.

Essential notes

Hitler occupied himself in prison, writing *Mein Kampf* ('My Struggle'). Part autobiography, part political tract, it is the fullest statement Hitler made of his world-view.

Essential notes

Under the *Führerprinzip* party members were required to obey their immediate superior without question. This meant that no one within the party, however senior, was permitted to challenge Hitler's decisions as leader.

with a view to establishing a base in the Reichstag, from which a final assault on power could be made.

In order to equip the NSDAP to fight election campaigns, it was reorganised into 35 regions (or *Gaue*) with boundaries corresponding to those of Weimar Germany's 35 electoral districts. Each *Gaue* was headed by a *Gauleiter* (regional leader).

Nazi ideology

Nazism was not a coherent philosophy. It was a jumble of instincts and prejudices. At its heart were ultra-nationalism and racism.

Nazi ideology: a summary

Ultra-nationalism	Racism	Authoritarianism	Anti-capitalism
A key Nazi assumption, derived from Social Darwinist thinking, was that nations engaged in competition for survival. A further assumption was that a citizen's most fundamental duty was to serve the nation. The specific objectives arising out of Nazi ultra-nationalism were revision of the Versailles Treaty, the creation of a 'Greater Germany' containing all the German-speaking peoples of Europe and a 'drive to the east' at the expense of Soviet Russia.	The Nazis subscribed fully to the two basic tenets of racism: mankind was divided into biologically distinct groups and some groups were superior to others. The Nazis did not distinguish sharply between race and nation: their preferred concept was the *Volk*, which incorporated elements of both. At the top of the Nazis' racial hierarchy was the Aryan (Nordic) master-race to which Germans belonged; at the bottom were the Slavs, viewed by the Nazis as *Untermenschen* (sub-human).	Hitler had only contempt for democracy, believing it to be an impediment to national unity because it promoted conflict between different elements within the nation. Nazis argued that if Germany was to succeed in its struggle for survival it had to be ruled in unsentimental fashion by an all-powerful leader. Nazis had no qualms about using force to subdue their critics and enemies.	Significant elements within the NSDAP were deeply hostile to big business. Leading Nazi anti-capitalists included Gregor Strasser and SA boss Ernst Röhm. Nazi anti-capitalists aimed to prevent the *Mittelstand* being squeezed between big business on one side and organised labour on the other. The flow of anti-capitalist rhetoric from within the NSDAP was one of the main reasons why the business community viewed it warily. Hitler never took the anti-capitalist dimension of Nazism seriously.

Essential notes

One reason for the Nazis' poor showing in the 1928 election was their ill-conceived 'urban plan', under which priority was given to an attempt to prise working-class voters away from the SPD and KPD. The new political strategy did not bear immediate fruit. In the 1928 Reichstag elections the NSDAP won only 800 000 votes and 12 seats.

Essential notes

There was a lot of common ground, ideologically speaking, between the Nazis and the conservative elites. Both were ultra-nationalist, anti-democratic, anti-communist and anti-Semitic. However, the Nazis, unlike the conservative elites, were not monarchists and had no great interest in regaining Germany's lost overseas colonies. For their part, the conservative elites were uneasy about a movement that described its philosophy as National Socialism.

Growing support: the Nazi electoral breakthrough

The economic context: impact of the slump in town and country, 1929–33

The agricultural sector of the German economy was in a depressed condition before 1929. Falling world food prices reduced the incomes of German farmers and forced them into debt. From 1927 onwards, the Nazis targeted rural voters, intensifying their efforts after their disappointing overall showing in the 1928 Reichstag elections.

The Nazis' electoral breakthrough took place against the background of the post-1929 economic slump. In Germany, as elsewhere, the slump meant business failures, falling output, rising unemployment, short-time working and wage cuts for those in work, deflation (falling prices) and intense pressure on government finances (receipts fell as the economy contracted).

Germany was hit harder than any of its European neighbours by the world depression. In 1932 unemployment reached 6 million (30 per cent of the workforce). Worst affected were areas of heavy industry such as the Ruhr and Hamburg. In some places one in two workers lost their jobs by 1932.

Unemployment in Germany rose sharply for a number of reasons:

- The withdrawal of US loans put huge strains on German banks, causing some to collapse. Companies found it extremely hard to borrow money and some were forced out of business as a result.

- The economic downturn in the USA and Britain deprived Germany of its chief export markets.

- Falling prices meant that would-be buyers delayed their purchases in the expectation that prices would fall further. Behaviour of this kind meant reduced demand for goods and further job losses.

The Nazi electoral breakthrough: who voted Nazi?

A study of two types of evidence relating to Reichstag elections in the years 1919–32 gives clear pointers to the kinds of voter who turned to the Nazis in and after 1930. These were:

- trends in support for the different political parties over time

- the geography of Reichstag elections.

Trends over time

In 1919–32, the Centre Party share of the vote in Reichstag elections was stable at around 20 per cent. This suggests that Catholic voters were for the most part resistant to the appeal of Nazism.

The SPD vote was more erratic than that of the Centre Party, but it clearly retained much of its hold on the working-class vote during the period of the Nazi electoral breakthrough. This suggests that the Nazis failed to win over the majority of working-class voters in the early 1930s.

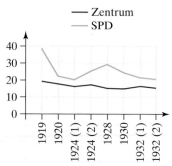
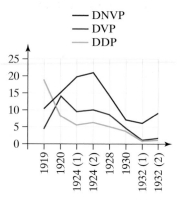

Support for the established middle-class parties (the DVP and DDP) collapsed in the early 1930s, suggesting that middle-class voters defected to the Nazis in large numbers. The DNVP also appears to have lost support to the Nazis.

Electoral geography

A study of the geography of Reichstag elections points in the same direction as a study of trends in support for different parties over time. Support for the Nazis during their breakthrough period was significantly weaker in Catholic regions (such as Bavaria and the Rhineland) and in industrial areas (such as Berlin and Saxony) than it was elsewhere.

The geography of the Nazi vote in the July 1932 Reichstag election

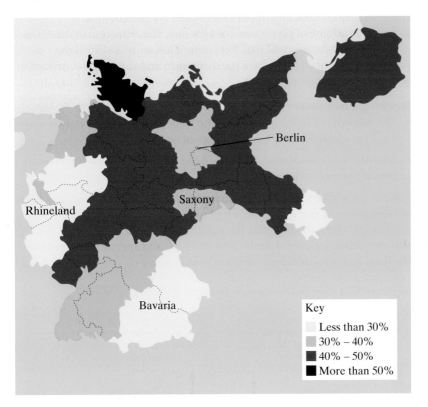

Key
Less than 30%
30% – 40%
40% – 50%
More than 50%

Examiners' notes

Three points to note, regarding the slump in Germany:

1. The official figure of 6 million understates the problem, as it does not include those in agriculture and retailing, with little income but not officially unemployed.
2. Unemployment did not jump from nothing to 6 million overnight in 1929: it rose steadily from just under 2 million to 6 million over a period of nearly four years.
3. In the slump, prices did not rise (inflation) but fell (deflation) because demand collapsed. In 1932 prices in Germany were around 30 per cent lower than they had been in 1914.

Note as well that official statistics under estimated the level of unemployment: the true figure in late 1932 may have been close to 8 million.

Narrowing the geographical focus from regions to particular neighbourhoods in Berlin offers a further insight into the Nazi vote: the Nazis attracted working-class voters in significant numbers. By 1932, for example, around one in five voters in Neukölln and Wedding, two working-class districts in Berlin, were supporting the Nazis. Although levels of support for the Nazis in these districts were nothing like as high as they were in affluent Berlin suburbs such as Zehlendorf and Wilmersdorf, this shows that the Nazis were capable of making serious electoral inroads even in deprived inner-city areas.

👉 **Continued on the next two pages**

The rise of the Nazis

Essential notes

The Nazis' commitment
to national renewal was
expressed in their slogan
Deutschland Erwache!
(Germany Awake!).

Examiners' notes

Be prepared for questions
that identify one cause of the
Nazi electoral breakthrough
and ask you to assess its
importance in relation to
others; for example: 'The
main reason for the Nazi
electoral breakthrough was
the effectiveness of Nazi
propaganda. How far do
you agree?'

The Communist menace

Essential notes

The SPD (in particular) and
the KPD were more than
political parties: they offered
their supporters an entire
lifestyle, including leisure and
cultural opportunities and
welfare provision. This helps
to explain the exceptional
loyalty of their supporters.

Why did people vote Nazi in the early 1930s?

Middle-class and upper-class voters

- Disillusioned and despairing middle- and upper-class voters were susceptible to the appeal of a party that was untainted by involvement in the Republic's failures and which offered the hope of national renewal.

- Hard-pressed farmers and *Mittelstand* voters may have found Nazi promises to protect them from financial ruin persuasive.

Fear of communism, however, was the most important reason why middle-class and upper-class voters turned to the Nazis. Between 1928 and 1932 the KPD vote nearly doubled. In addition, communist paramilitaries were an increasingly visible presence on the streets of Germany's major cities. To middle-class and upper-class voters the possibility of a communist seizure of power seemed very real. The attraction of the Nazis in these circumstances was that they, more than anyone else on the political right, appeared to have the dynamism and ruthlessness needed to eliminate the communist threat.

Working-class voters

- The minority of German workers who were political conservatives may have been enthused by Nazi promises of national revival.

- Some of the unemployed may have been impressed by the Nazi vow to provide 'work and bread'.

Most of the workers who voted Nazi in the early 1930s appear to have been self-employed or non-unionised employees in small factories or workshops. They stood outside the highly organised and close-knit sub-cultures associated with the SPD and KPD and appear to have shared the fears and insecurities of the lower-middle classes.

Summary: Who voted Nazi in the early 1930s?

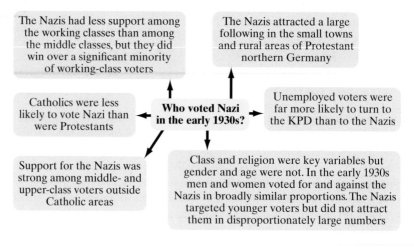

Nazi organisation and propaganda

The Nazis clearly benefited from the sense of unease and panic that arose out of economic crisis, but they did not, of course, stand idly by while votes fell into their lap. They exploited the opportunity they were given with energy and skill.

The Nazis depicted themselves as a *Volkspartei* ('people's party') with the aim of furthering the interests of the nation as a whole. Other political parties, they claimed, were sectional in character, intent on furthering the interests only of a section of the community.

At the same time, the Nazis targeted a range of different groups in society and fashioned a distinctive appeal to each of them. By using this tactic, they turned themselves into 'a catch-all party of protest' (Thomas Childers, *The Nazi Vote*, 1983) or 'a rainbow coalition of the discontented' (Richard Evans, *The Coming of the Third Reich*, 2004).

Organisationally, the Nazis transformed themselves into a formidable vote-winning machine. Apart from the increasingly well-staffed *Gaue* organisations, they set up units within the party that focused on the demands and grievances of all sorts of groups, among them civil servants, ex-servicemen and factory workers. An example of such a unit is R.W. Darrés' Agricultural Apparatus, founded in 1930 to target the rural vote.

The Nazis campaigned with ferocious energy in the elections of the early 1930s, holding more meetings and producing more campaign literature than their opponents.

Under the direction of Josef Goebbels, the party's propaganda chief from 1930 onwards, the Nazis outclassed their opponents in terms of getting their message across in imaginative, attention-grabbing ways. Rallies, parades and processions were a Nazi speciality.

One of the Nazis' trump cards in propaganda terms was Hitler himself. Many who heard him speak in the early 1930s went away spellbound and convinced of his sincerity.

These figures show the speed and scale of the Nazi electoral breakthrough in the early 1930s as measured by number and percentage share of the vote won, and number of Reichstag seats won.

Essential notes

Examples of promises made by the Nazis to different groups in elections in the early 1930s include:

- farmers – protection against food imports from abroad
- shopkeepers – action to eliminate the threat posed to the livelihood of small retailers by department stores
- pensioners – increased benefits
- unemployed workers – a massive government-sponsored job-creation scheme
- businessmen – proper rewards for enterprise.

The Nazis, observes the German historian Bernd Weisbrod, 'promised almost anything to everybody'.

The Nazi electoral breakthrough: statistics

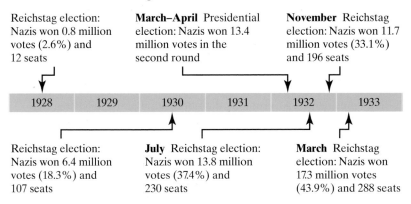

Reichstag election: Nazis won 0.8 million votes (2.6%) and 12 seats

March–April Presidential election: Nazis won 13.4 million votes in the second round

November Reichstag election: Nazis won 11.7 million votes (33.1%) and 196 seats

| 1928 | 1929 | 1930 | 1931 | 1932 | 1933 |

Reichstag election: Nazis won 6.4 million votes (18.3%) and 107 seats

July Reichstag election: Nazis won 13.8 million votes (37.4%) and 230 seats

March Reichstag election: Nazis won 17.3 million votes (43.9%) and 288 seats

Presidential government, 1930–3

The breakdown of parliamentary government, 1930

Between 1919 and 1930 Germany was governed by administrations that remained in office as long as they commanded the support of the majority of the Reichstag. In 1930 two developments made parliamentary government of this kind impossible:

- Herman Müller's 'grand coalition', which had been in office since 1928, broke up. The cause was the budget deficit that arose out of the slump (tax revenues fell sharply as levels of economic activity declined). The non-socialist parties in Müller's government favoured reducing the deficit through cuts in unemployment benefit. The SPD disagreed, unwilling to see its unemployed supporters suffer while the better-off were making no contribution to deficit reduction. The breakdown in relations between the SPD and the non-socialist moderate parties meant that after the fall of Müller's coalition no new government responsible to the Reichstag could be formed. A 'middle-class coalition' of DVP, DDP and Centre was a non-runner because together the three parties controlled fewer than 30 per cent of Reichstag seats.

- In the subsequent 1930 elections the moderates lost ground and the extremists (NSDAP and KPD) made gains. The four 'democratic' parties (SPD, DDP, Centre, DVP) between them did not now command a majority in the Reichstag. Even if they had been able to overcome their differences it would not have been possible for them to form a workable four-party coalition government.

Presidential government: phase one, 1930–2

The alternative to parliamentary government was 'presidential government' in which the President used his powers under Article 48 to rule by decree.

The nature of 'presidential government'

The advent of 'presidential government' meant that the anti-Republican right was back in control of Germany. Hindenburg himself was an anti-Republican who despised parliamentary democracy. All members of his '*camarilla*' of close advisers were also strongly anti-Republican. Its leading figures included his army-officer son Oskar and Otto Meissner, top civil servant in the President's secretariat. Most influential of all, however, was the clever, unscrupulous and ambitious General Kurt von Schleicher, who spoke for the army.

Hindenburg and his *camarilla* did not govern Germany on a day-to-day basis themselves. This task was entrusted to a new Chancellor, Heinrich Brüning, a scholarly but colourless financial expert and a right-wing member of the Centre Party.

Initially 'presidential government' did not mean that the Reichstag was completely marginalised. Brüning was a member of the Reichstag and kept lines to his Reichstag colleagues open. He received support from the middle-class parties while the SPD tolerated presidential government because there was no alternative to it. As time went on, though, the Reichstag became increasingly irrelevant.

Essential notes

Camarilla is a word of Spanish origin and is used to refer to a group of courtiers or favourites who surround a king or ruler.

The marginalisation of the Reichstag

	1930	1931	1932
Number of days in session	94	42	13
Number of laws passed	98	34	5
Decrees issued under Article 48	5	44	66

In the early days of 'presidential government' the Nazis were not seen by Hindenburg's *camarilla* as a key element in the political equation. Their 107 seats in the Reichstag did not give them decisive leverage. In addition, Hindenburg had little time for the Nazis, seeing them as little better than hooligans and dismissing Hitler as 'the Austrian corporal'.

Brüning's economic policies
Brüning was an orthodox, unimaginative economic thinker who thought that the economy would eventually recover of its own accord. In the meantime his priority was ensuring the state did not go bankrupt. He sought to reduce the budget deficit by increasing taxes and cutting public spending, including welfare benefits.

The army and the *Junkers* received preferential treatment. Spending on the army was not cut and *Junkers* continued to receive generous agricultural subsidies through the *Osthilfe* ('eastern aid') scheme.

Brüning used the world economic crisis to rid Germany of the burden of reparations. Payments were suspended by international agreement in 1931 and scrapped altogether in 1932.

Brüning's austerity policies sucked demand out of the economy and made unemployment worse. He acquired the nickname of 'the Hunger Chancellor'.

Brüning's downfall, May 1932
In early 1932 Hindenburg and the *camarilla* lost confidence in Brüning because:

- the economy was deteriorating
- disorder and street violence were worsening.

Brüning botched an attempt to persuade the Reichstag to extend Hindenburg's term in office as President (which expired in 1932) in order to relieve him of the need to seek re-election. To make matters worse, Hitler stood against Hindenburg when the Presidential election was held (March 1932), depriving him of an overall majority on the first ballot and forcing a second, run-off contest between the leading candidates. Hindenburg won on the second ballot by 19 million votes to Hitler's 13 million, but Hitler mopped up the right-wing vote, leaving Hindenburg (to his fury) reliant on the votes of Catholics and Social Democrats.

In May 1932 it became known in *Junker* circles that members of Brüning's cabinet were working on a scheme to buy up insolvent *Junker* estates and settle unemployed workers on them. Outraged *Junkers* complained to Hindenburg that Brüning was an 'agrarian Bolshevik'. It was the final straw. Brüning was dismissed soon afterwards.

Essential notes

Nazis and communists killed in street fighting, 1930–2

	Communists	Nazis
1930	44	17
1931	52	42
1932	75	84

☞ **Continued on the next two pages**

Essential notes

Franz von Papen came from a family of Catholic aristocrats. At the time of his appointment as Chancellor he was a political unknown: he was not a member of the Reichstag but of the Prussian *Landtag*. Britain's ambassador to Germany described him as 'a man of second-rate ability – a lightweight'.

Presidential government: phase two, 1932–3

Schleicher woos Hitler

In 1932 Schleicher, the most influential of Hindenburg's advisers, decided that Germany's deepening crisis called for the introduction of a more extreme form of 'presidential government' than what had operated over the previous two years. He now aimed to sideline the Reichstag permanently and establish a system of free-standing Presidential rule, backed by the conservative elites and the Nazis. The Nazis featured in Schleicher's thinking because he needed insurance against the charge that his plans involved imposing authoritarian rule on Germany against its will: the Nazis could provide an appearance of mass support.

In mid-1932 Schleicher set out to woo Hitler:

- A far right Chancellor (Franz von Papen) was installed, with a number of far right ministers to serve under him ('the cabinet of barons').

- The ban Brüning had imposed on the SA was lifted.

- Reichstag elections were called, giving the Nazis an opportunity to strengthen their electoral base.

- In flagrant violation of the constitution, von Papen deposed the Social Democratic state government of Prussia – a government that had been a determined opponent of Nazism.

Hitler's refusal to join the government, August 1932

In the elections of July 1932, the Nazis won 37.4 per cent of the vote and became the largest single party in the Reichstag. After the elections there was an intensive round of talks, involving Hitler, Schleicher, von Papen and Hindenburg, which culminated in Hitler refusing to serve under von Papen and demanding the Chancellorship for himself. Hindenburg, whose low opinion of Hitler was unchanged, sent him packing.

Jockeying for position, late 1932

The failure of the August talks was followed by a period in which those who had been centrally involved jockeyed for position.

Hitler	Angry at being snubbed by Hindenburg, Hitler took his revenge by ordering the Nazi delegation in the Reichstag to join other parties in passing a vote of no-confidence in the von Papen government, forcing a further Reichstag election.
	This move backfired: in the November elections the Nazis won 2 million fewer votes than in July. The defectors were right-wing voters annoyed by what they saw as Hitler's selfish refusal to work under von Papen.
Von Papen	Exploiting his close personal friendship with Hindenburg, von Papen tried to persuade the President to establish a 'New State' under which he as Chancellor would be given dictatorial powers.
Schleicher	Having no further use for von Papen and exasperated by the way he had developed ambitions of his own, Schleicher talked Hindenburg into dismissing him, insisting that this was what the army wanted.

Schleicher's Chancellorship, December 1932–January 1933

Schleicher preferred to operate from behind the scenes, but in the absence of any other plausible candidate he now took over the Chancellorship himself. His problem was that he was short of allies and had little support in the country at large. In desperation, he tried to persuade the anti-capitalist or Strasserite wing of the NSDAP and SPD trades unionists to join him in an effort to bring down unemployment. He even offered Gregor Strasser the Vice-Chancellorship. But his scheme was a non-starter: the Nazis were not easily split and the SPD were never going to collaborate with the Nazis.

Hitler, Hindenburg and von Papen, January 1933

In early 1933 each of the three had incentives to do a deal:

- Hitler was under pressure from his followers after the disappointing November election result. In addition he was angered by Schleicher's attempt to split the NSDAP and wanted revenge.

- A deal with the Nazis offered von Papen a way back into office.

- Hindenburg wanted von Papen back alongside him in government and was willing to overcome his distaste for Hitler in order to bring this about.

Under the agreement reached in January 1933, Hitler became Chancellor with von Papen as his Vice-Chancellor. Von Papen was confident that he could control Hitler. He told friends that he had 'hired' Hitler and would soon have him 'pushed into a corner'.

The political crisis of 1932–3

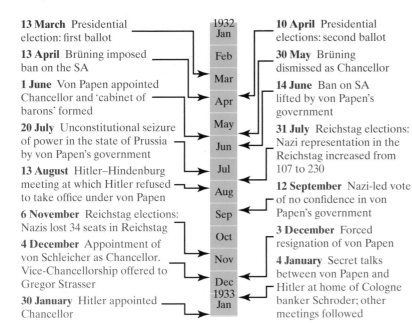

The Nazi seizure of power, 1933

Hitler's position in January 1933

When Hitler became Chancellor he acquired considerable but not absolute power. With 230 out of 584 seats in the Reichstag following the November 1932 elections, the Nazis were 63 short of an overall majority.

Hitler was thus dependent on Hindenburg just as Brüning, von Papen and Schleicher had been before him. Hitler's government was a coalition in which only three out of 12 ministers were Nazis.

Hitler's aim now was to end 'presidential government' and concentrate power in his own hands – without, however, acting unconstitutionally. This meant a further Reichstag election. Hindenburg had already agreed to use his power to dissolve the Reichstag and force an election.

Hitler's objective in the election was not just an overall majority but the two-thirds majority in the Reichstag required to amend the 1919 Constitution.

The 1933 election campaign

Desperate for victory, the Nazis used every tactic open to them short of outright ballot-rigging. Violence and intimidation were widespread. In the course of the five-week campaign, 69 people were killed.

The 1933 election campaign: key events

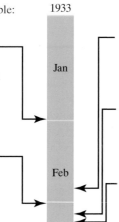

31 January Appeal to the German people: Hitler opened the campaign with a declaration blaming the communists for Germany's troubles and depicting his government as the spearhead of a 'national uprising' which would restore Germany to greatness.

22 February SA enrolled as special constables: Goering recruited 50 000 auxiliary policemen, mostly from the SA, ostensibly to maintain order during the election campaign but in reality to legalise Nazi thuggery.

17 February Goering's police order: In his capacity as newly appointed Prussian Interior Minister, Goering warned policemen that they would face disciplinary action if they failed to open fire on anyone involved in 'communist terrorist acts'.

27 February Reichstag fire: An arson attack on the parliament building by a Dutch communist, Marinus van der Lubbe, enabled the Nazis to launch an anti-communist propaganda offensive in the final days of the campaign.

28 February Decree for Protection of the People and the State: The KPD was effectively outlawed. Basic rights guaranteed by the 1919 Constitution – freedom of speech, assembly and association – were suspended indefinitely (sometimes referred to as the Reichstag Fire Decree).

Results of the March 1933 election

At first sight the result was disappointing from the Nazi point of view. The Nazis won 44 per cent of the vote, giving them 288 out of a total of 647 Reichstag seats – 36 short of the 324 needed for an overall majority.

The result was more favourable to the Nazis than it appeared. Because the KPD had been outlawed, its 81 deputies could not take their seats. Moreover, the DNVP were now allied to the NSDAP (they were soon to merge with it), meaning that their 52 seats could be added to the Nazi total. The Nazi–DNVP bloc thus controlled 340 seats in a Reichstag with an effective membership of 566 – well over the 284 needed for an overall majority.

The Nazi–DNVP bloc was 92 seats short of the 432 needed for a two-thirds majority and the power to amend the 1919 Constitution that went with it.

The Enabling Law, 23 March 1933

When the Reichstag assembled after the 1933 election Hitler put before it an Enabling Law (formally known as the 'Law for the Removal of Distress from People and the Reich'). Its purpose was to allow the government to introduce new laws and to amend the 1919 Constitution without the approval of either the President or the Reichstag – in short, to turn Germany into a dictatorship in which Hitler could rule by decree.

The Social Democrats were irreconcilably opposed to the Enabling Law, but the Centre Party decided, after a heated intra-party debate, to support it. Centre Party leaders, concerned above all to safeguard the position of the Catholic Church in Germany, were ready to accept Hitler's undertakings about its future (freedom of worship, preservation of Catholic schools and youth movements) at face value.

The Enabling Law was passed by the Reichstag by 444–94 votes.

After the passage of the Enabling Law the Nazis took further steps in the spring and summer of 1933 to tighten their control over Germany:

- *Political parties*: The SPD was banned (June 1933) and other political parties voluntarily wound themselves down (June–July 1933). The KPD had effectively been outlawed in March 1933.

- *Trades unions*: The free trades unions were broken up; premises were occupied, leaders arrested and funds seized (May 1933).

- *The Länder*: A law passed in April 1933 empowered central government to appoint Reich Commissioners (usually the local *Gauleiter*) to run the states.

- *Civil service*: Political undesirables and Jews were dismissed under the 'Law for the Restoration of Professional Civil Service' (April 1933), though Hindenburg secured an exemption for Jewish war veterans.

- *Police*: Police chiefs hostile to Nazism were dismissed in 1933.

- *Press*: Communist and SPD newspapers were closed down in 1933.

Violence and terror, 1933

The Nazi seizure of power was not just an exercise in high politics. It also involved a great deal of violence at grass-roots level. The perpetrators of violence were SA units acting on their own initiative, without direct orders from the top. The victims of this localised SA terror were the political left (communists and Social Democrats) and Jews. Homes and offices were ransacked, individuals were beaten, arrested, tortured and killed.

Individuals arrested by the SA in early 1933 were usually taken to makeshift camps set up in disused buildings. When Hitler stopped the SA rampage, because protests against it became too loud to ignore, these so-called 'wild camps' were shut down and replaced by concentration camps for political detainees run by Himmler's SS. The camp at Dachau, near Munich, was the model on which others (around 80 in all) were based.

Examiners' notes

When explaining electoral support for the Nazis, do not focus exclusively on their use of terror. It can be argued that Nazi success was to a considerable extent the result of the fears of many Germans of the communist threat. They did not want the oppressiveness and brutality of Stalin's regime to be replicated in Germany.

Examiners' notes

A question worth considering is the extent to which the Nazis came to power by legal means.

The Nazis repeatedly declared their commitment to 'legality' after 1925 and January–March 1933 observed the letter, if not the spirit, of the 1919 Constitution. On the other hand, from 1925 onwards they used street violence in a calculated way to destabilise the Republic. Two of the worst examples of Nazi-inspired violence were 'Bloody Sunday' at Altona in June 1932 (18 killed in SA–communist clashes) and the 'Potempa incident' in August 1932 (a young communist beaten to death in front of his young family).

Essential notes

Survey evidence on attitudes to Nazi rule (based on questionnaires completed in the 1980s by a cross-section of 3000 people who had lived through the Nazi era)

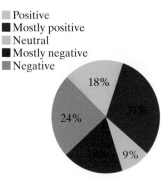

■ Positive
■ Mostly positive
■ Neutral
■ Mostly negative
■ Negative

(Source: E. Johnson and K.H. Reuband, *What We Knew: Terror, Mass Murder and Everyday Life in Nazi Germany*, 2005)

Examiners' notes

When analysing Section B sources you need to identify those parts of an interpretation that are contentious – open to challenge on the basis of the other sources or your own knowledge – and those that are not. Here, for example, what LeBor and Boyes say about resistance is uncontentious because they carefully refer to 'organised' resistance, but their claim that working-class acceptance of Nazi rule was secured by a 'reward' system rather than terror is highly debatable.

How popular was the Nazi regime?

The study of popular attitudes towards Nazism in the 1930s is a difficult undertaking. Obviously there was no single uniform German attitude towards the Nazi regime. Instead, there was a spectrum of attitudes ranging from enthusiasm through acquiescence out to active hostility. Moreover, at the individual level it was possible to have mixed feelings, welcoming some aspects of Nazi rule and disliking others. In these circumstances, historians have asked a number of questions about popular attitudes towards Nazism – without, however, coming up with agreed answers:

- How extensive was enthusiasm for Nazi rule? In which sections of society was enthusiasm most likely to be found?

- How is 'resistance' to Nazism to be defined? How much resistance, however defined, was there to Nazi rule in the 1930s?

- How is acquiescence to be explained? Were Germans, as one early commentator on the Third Reich (Konrad Heiden, *The Führer*, 1944) put it, 'enslaved' by Hitler – that is, cowed into submission by Nazi terror? Or is the German historian Hans-Ulrich Wehler correct when he maintains: 'it is mistaken to characterise the Führer state as a terror regime in which a band of desperadoes exercised a kind of alien rule to which the decent but defenceless majority had to bow'?

Source 1
(From Adam LeBor and Roger Boyes, *Seduced by Hitler*, published by Sourcebooks 2000)

Until the last year of the war the regime managed to secure the active or passive support of many sections of the middle classes and the various elites. Organized resistance was confined to the nooks and crannies of society. The question is why did the working class – the most aggrieved sector of society – not launch at least one major challenge to the regime? Without minimizing the use of terror, we believe that Hitler's success in winning over the working class was due to a sophisticated reward system, that sufficient numbers of workers were seduced to neutralize resistance.

Enthusiasm for Nazi rule

Historical research, some of it based on survey evidence, leaves little doubt that there was a substantial amount of genuine enthusiasm for Nazi rule in the 1930s. It is clear, too, that the people most likely to have been positive about Nazism were (unsurprisingly) those who had voted Nazi in pre-1933 elections: middle-class and upper-class Protestants. Nothing Hitler did after 1933 disappointed or alienated such people.

Why were the middle and upper classes enthusiasts for Nazi rule?

In the early 1930s Germany's conservative elites and middle classes were terrified of a communist seizure of power. In and after 1933, Hitler destroyed the KPD as an organised political force and, by doing so, earned the lasting gratitude of the propertied classes.

The Nazis were able to claim victory in what they called the 'battle for labour': by 1936 unemployment in Germany was down to just over 1 million, having been 6 million when Hitler became Chancellor. Middle-class Germans had not been as badly hit by the economic slump as the working classes but they took pride in the fact that Germany had been put back on its feet.

Hitler's assertive foreign policy was warmly received by middle-class and upper-class nationalists. In the 1930s there was a string of foreign policy successes to celebrate: reoccupation of the Rhineland (1936), union with Austria (1938), the seizure of the Sudetenland from Czechoslovakia (1938) and the occupation of the remainder of Czechoslovakia (1939).

Many middle-class Germans initially welcomed the Nazis' hard-line youth policies (the emphasis on physical activity in schools, military-style training in the Hitler Youth, compulsory labour service in the RAD) as a return to sanity after Weimar decadence. Opinion was to change when a decline in academic standards became apparent.

Goebbels' propaganda operation in the 1930s successfully projected Hitler as a leader above party, the leader of the national community (*Volksgemeinschaft*). This is what historian Ian Kershaw has called 'the Hitler Myth'. As a result of Goebbels' propaganda campaign Hitler was, in the 1930s, markedly more popular than his party.

Young people and Nazism

Hitler attached huge importance to winning over the younger generation to National Socialism:

- He needed people who were willing to fight and die for Nazism on the battlefield.

- He wanted to ensure the regime's long-term survival. ('I tell you the Nazi movement will go on for 1000 years.')

Young people were therefore subjected to systematic indoctrination. The National Socialist school curriculum prioritised 'racial science', physical education and the Nazis' interpretation of Germany's recent history. In the evenings and at weekends the young were fed a diet of *Wehrsport* ('military athletics') and Nazi propaganda through the Hitler Youth movement. Indoctrination had its effect: it is not a coincidence that many of the German soldiers who committed war crimes in Poland and Russia in the 1939–45 war came from the generation that grew to adulthood in the 1930s.

Essential notes

The RAD was the *Reichsarbeitsdienst* or National Labour Service. In 1935 it became compulsory for 18–25-year-old men to do six months' service in the RAD. Usually it involved working on construction projects.

Hitler expressed his aims for youth as follows, in 1939:

> A violently active, dominating, intrepid, brutal youth – that is what I am after. It must be indifferent to pain. There must be no weakness or tenderness in it.'

Essential notes

Indoctrination is the process of getting someone to believe something so completely that nothing will shake that belief.

Essential notes

A broad definition of 'resistance' was adopted by Munich's Institute of Contemporary History in 1973 in connection with a major research project: 'Resistance is understood as every form of active or passive behaviour which involved rejection of the National Socialist regime or a part of National Socialist ideology and was bound up with certain risks.'

Essential notes

An alternative to the *Widerstand/Resistenz* distinction is to think of resistance as a pyramid, with a small number of active resisters (people who totally rejected Nazism and aimed to overthrow the regime) at the top. Beneath them is a larger category of opponents (people who opposed particular Nazi policies without necessarily rejecting the regime as a whole) and at the base of the pyramid is a category of non-conformists (people who neither resisted nor opposed the regime but who, in various ways, failed to conform to its demands).

Resistance to Nazism

The problem of definition

The term 'resistance' is problematic because it is a word that can be used to cover a wide range of behaviours:

- In the 1950s and 1960s historians worked on the basis that 'resistance' meant either organised attempts to bring down the Nazi regime (such as the 'bomb plot' of 1944) or acts of protest provoked by particular Nazi actions or policies (such as the public attack on the Nazis' T-4 Euthanasia programme by Clemens von Galen, the Catholic Bishop of Münster, in 1941).

- In the 1970s, as historians became more interested in ordinary people and everyday life, there were suggestions that the definition needed to be broadened to include minor acts of dissent at the grass-roots level (such as refusing to give the 'Heil Hitler!' salute) or the phenomenon of 'inner retreat' (in which people who rejected Nazi values withdrew into private and family life).

- The German historian Martin Broszat usefully distinguished between *Widerstand* and *Resistenz*. By *Widerstand* he meant active resistance – resistance as understood by the historians of the 1950s and 1960s. By *Resistenz* he meant passive resistance, a refusal to accept Nazi values, which sometimes found expression in acts of dissent.

Active resistance in the 1930s

There was very little active resistance (*Widerstand*) to the Nazi regime in the 1930s. What resistance there was came from the remnants of the left-wing parties, the Christian Churches and dissident youth movements.

SPD and KPD

The SPD and KPD were overwhelmed by the ferocity of the Nazi onslaught on them in 1933. Their organisations were smashed and their leaders either arrested or forced to flee abroad. Any sort of open confrontation with the Nazi regime was out of the question. Both parties set their sights no higher than keeping going in some form until the Nazi regime collapsed.

The SPD in exile (SOPADE) maintained an underground information-gathering network in Germany. In addition there was distribution of underground leaflets and an illegal newspaper, *Sozialistische Aktion* (estimated circulation 200 000).

The KPD also distributed leaflets. More audaciously, in 1937 it set up (at the behest of Soviet Russia's intelligence services) a spy network known by the Nazis as the *Rote Kapelle* ('Red Orchestra'). The Red Orchestra survived for five years before being broken up by the SS.

The Christian Churches

The leading Protestant resisters were Martin Niemöller and Dietrich Bonhöffer, who established the Confessional Church in response to the Nazi takeover of the Evangelical Churches. In all, some 800 (out of 17 000) Protestant pastors were arrested by the Nazis.

Individual Catholic priests condemned Nazism and in 1937 there was popular protest in Oldenburg when the Nazis attempted to remove crucifixes from school classrooms. In 1937, the Pope, who in 1933 had agreed a 'concordat' with Hitler, issued a statement entitled 'With burning concern' in protest against Hitler's treatment of the Catholic Church.

There were limits to the scope of Christian resistance. It centred on defence of the Churches and their interests and did not involve a wholesale rejection of Nazism. In 1936, for example, Bishop von Galen of Munster, wartime protestor against Nazi euthanasia programmes, asked for God's blessing on Hitler's endeavours after the reoccupation of the Rhineland.

Youth protest

Several youth protest movements appeared in the late 1930s. Only a small minority of German young people were involved:

- The 'Swing Kids', middle-class in origin, resented being regimented in the Hitler Youth and expressed their individuality by wearing their hair long and listening to jazz (which the Nazis viewed as 'degenerate' music). The 'Swing Kids' were an example of *Resistenz* rather than *Widerstand*.

- The 'Edelweiss Pirates', a loose alliance of gangs of working-class youths based in the industrial regions of western Germany, were more aggressive and politicised than the 'Swing Kids'. Adopting the slogan 'Eternal War on the Hitler Youth', they ambushed Hitler Youth patrols and beat up Hitler Youth members. The Nazi regime's response was draconian: arrests, detention in concentration camps and, in the case of some ringleaders, execution.

Why was there so little resistance to Nazism in the 1930s?

- The Nazi regime was actively supported by many Germans.

- Nazi efforts to 'depoliticise' everyday life in 1930s Germany and therefore to neutralise potential dissidents had considerable success.

- The organisational frameworks of the most potential centres of opposition (the SPD and KPD) were broken up in 1933.

- Potential leaders of resistance were either imprisoned in concentration camps or in exile abroad.

- The security policing operation run by Himmler and Heydrich was highly efficient.

- The penalties for resistance or dissent were known to be severe.

- The *Rote Kapelle* apart, anti-Nazi resisters received little help or support from abroad.

Examiners' notes

Nazi efforts to distract people's attention from political issues are important in examination terms and are considered more fully in the pages that follow.

Essential notes

Alternative terms used to describe this attitude of acquiescence are 'consent', 'conformity' and 'acceptance'.

Essential notes

Gleichschaltung literally means 'the process of switching on to the same wavelength' or 'bringing into line'. In the context of 1930s Germany it is used to refer to the abolition or Nazification of the country's major institutions.

Consent and conformity

Between the minority of active resisters and the much larger number of enthusiasts for Nazi rule there was, in 1930s Germany, a broad swathe of opinion whose attitude to Nazism was one of acceptance or conformity. People in this category were those who had not been favourably disposed towards the Nazis before 1933 – not only large parts of the working class but also Catholics and the more liberal elements within the middle classes.

Historians broadly agree that the Nazis secured acceptance and conformity through what Alan Bullock (*Hitler: A Study in Tyranny*, 1962) calls 'a combination of propaganda and terrorism'. Where they disagree is on the relative importance of the two. In order to offer well-formed judgements on this issue you will need a knowledge and understanding of both Nazi terror and Nazi propaganda.

Gleichschaltung: an outline

Political parties: After the outlawing of some political parties (KPD and SPD) and the 'voluntary' liquidation of others, a 'Law Against the Formation of New Parties' was introduced in July 1933.

The Länder: The Nazis took control of the individual states in April 1933 by appointing Reich Commissioners to run them and in 1934 formally abolished state parliaments and the *Reichsrat* through the 'Law for the Reconstruction of the State'.

Trades unions: After the Nazi break-up of free trades unions in May 1933, workers were required to join a Nazi organisation, the German Labour Front (DAF).

Institutions that were abolished because their continued existence was seen as incompatible with National Socialism

Army: The army retained the autonomy which it had enjoyed under the Weimar Republic and the *Kaiserreich*. It experienced little in the way of political interference until the later 1930s, though soldiers were required to take an oath of loyalty to Hitler (introduced 1934).

Press: Socialist and communist newspapers were banned, but most other national and local newspapers continued to appear. However, what they published was controlled by Goebbels' Propaganda Ministry.

Big business: Relations between the Nazis and big business were for the most part cordial. Employers' associations were merged to form the Reich Estate of German Industry, but it was not controlled by Nazi Party members.

Institutions that were allowed to remain in existence, but were modified to bring them firmly under Nazi control

Education: Control of schools was centralised and a new curriculum imposed from above.

Institutions that were largely left alone, either because they were too powerful to confront or because they were favourably disposed to Nazism

Political undesirables were purged from other professions besides the civil service – university teaching, school teaching, the judiciary and the legal profession.

Protestant Churches: Germany's Lutherans were organised into the German Evangelical Church headed by a 'Reich Bishop'. A dissident minority broke away to form the 'Confessional Church' (1934).

Roman Catholic Church: Under the 'concordat' (treaty) between the Vatican and the Nazis (July 1933) the Church agreed to abstain from political activity and in return was promised that its rights would be upheld.

Gleichschaltung, 1933–4

The actions the Nazis took in early 1933 to consolidate their hold on power – the elimination of other political parties, the liquidation of the trades union movement and the purging of undesirables from the civil service – were part of a broader process of *Gleichschaltung*, which aimed to neutralise potential centres of opposition and lasted into 1934. *Gleichschaltung* was not a uniform process: some institutions were destroyed, others were reformed and some were left largely undisturbed.

The 'Night of the Long Knives', 1934

In 1934 Hitler ruthlessly crushed dissent in his own ranks when he ordered the murder of the top SA leaders. This episode became known as 'The Night of the Long Knives'. The SA leadership, headed by Ernst Röhm, was a problem for three reasons:

1. The SA wanted to merge with the much smaller German army. Since the SA were street brawlers rather than trained soldiers, Hitler feared that a merger would undermine the effectiveness of Germany's armed forces.

2. The SA leaders were committed anti-capitalists. They began to call for a 'second revolution' (the first being the seizure of power in 1933) that would target big business. Hitler had no intention of waging war on Germany's industrial tycoons.

3. The SA leadership was an embarrassment. They openly led dissolute lifestyles at a time when millions of Germans were unemployed.

Hitler struck in June 1934. He ordered the murder of over fifty of the SA's top leaders, Röhm included. At the same time he settled some old scores: also murdered in June 1934 were Gustav von Kahr, Gregor Strasser and Kurt von Schleicher. All of the killings were carried out by Himmler's SS.

The SS police state

Historical writing about Nazism in the 1950s and 1960s was strongly influenced by the concept of totalitarianism. It was a concept used to highlight the similarities between the oppressive dictatorships of 20th-century Europe – single-party government, all-powerful leaders, an all-pervasive ideology and terroristic policing. Studies of Nazi Germany that draw upon the concept of totalitarianism emphasise the fact that it was, like Stalin's Russia, a police state that operated a 'system of terror' (Karl Dietrich Bracher, *The German Dictatorship*, 1969).

In the 1930s the SS became the principal instrument of Nazi oppression. It acquired responsibility for keeping watch on the German people, neutralising suspected enemies of the regime (usually by taking them into 'protective custody') and controlling an elaborate system of concentration camps. It grew so powerful that it became a state within a state. During the war it acquired even more power.

Essential notes

The 'Night of the Long Knives' was seen outside Germany as an act of political gangsterism but did not dent Hitler's popularity inside Germany: middle-class opinion seems to have taken the view that Hitler had acted appropriately to root out corrupt elements of the Nazi Party.

Essential notes

A police state can be defined as one in which a repressive government maintains control over political, social and economic life by means of police forces, especially secret police forces, that can operate outside the framework of the law.

Essential notes

Estimated total concentration camp population

1933	26 000
1934	9000
1935	5000
1936	10 000
1937	8000
1938	60 000

Continued on the next four pages

The growth of the SS in the 1930s

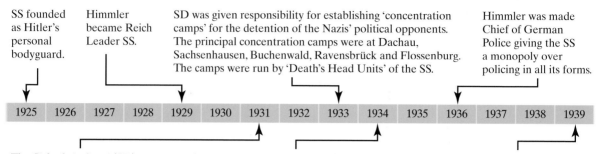

| SS founded as Hitler's personal bodyguard. | Himmler became Reich Leader SS. | SD was given responsibility for establishing 'concentration camps' for the detention of the Nazis' political opponents. The principal concentration camps were at Dachau, Sachsenhausen, Buchenwald, Ravensbrück and Flossenburg. The camps were run by 'Death's Head Units' of the SS. | Himmler was made Chief of German Police giving the SS a monopoly over policing in all its forms. |

| 1925 | 1926 | 1927 | 1928 | 1929 | 1930 | 1931 | 1932 | 1933 | 1934 | 1935 | 1936 | 1937 | 1938 | 1939 |

| The *Sicherheitsdienst* (SD) or 'Security Service' was created within the SS (an intelligence service for the Nazi Party, spying on its enemies, headed by Reinhard Heydrich). | After the 'Night of the Long Knives' (carried out by the SS) Himmler was given control of Germany's secret police force, the *Gestapo*, which the Nazis had created out of the political branch of the pre-1933 Prussian state police. The SD, a Nazi Party organisation, operated in parallel with the *Gestapo*. | The party-based SD, the state secret police (the *Gestapo*) and the ordinary criminal police were incorporated into a single body, the Reich Main Security Office (the RSHA). |

A population terrorised into submission?

In recent years historians have questioned the idea that in the 1930s Germans were subdued by a 'gigantic apparatus' (historian K.D. Bracher) of terror.

It has been suggested that the Nazis did not use terror as a means of controlling the entire nation but instead used it as a focused tool against perceived enemies of the regime. Some support for this suggestion is offered by what is known about the numbers of concentration camp detainees.

It has been pointed out that the *Gestapo* was in fact a relatively small organisation. In the late 1930s, for example, the 4 million people living in the Düsseldorf district of the Ruhr were watched over by a mere 300 *Gestapo* personnel. Nationally, the *Gestapo* had a staff of only 32 000. The SS in its entirety in the late 1930s numbered under a quarter of a million.

Essential notes

Total membership of the SS

1931	10 000
1933	52 000
1935	200 000
1939	240 000
1944	800 000*

* includes Waffen–SS (military units)

Source 2
(From Robert Gellately, *Backing Hitler: Consent and Coercion in Nazi Germany*, published by Oxford University Press 2001)

The regime made no bones about using coercion in many forms against its declared enemies, but it also sought the consent and support of the people at every turn. Coercion and terror were highly selective, and certainly did not rain down universally on the heads of the German people. By and large, terror was not needed to force the majority or even significant minorities into line. By the end of 1933, power was already secured, and the brutalities and violence that are identified with the so-called Nazi 'seizure of power' began to wane. Terror itself does not adequately explain how the Third Reich came to be, nor account for its considerable staying power.

Propaganda

Propaganda was the province of Goebbels' Ministry of Propaganda and National Enlightenment and its associated organisations.

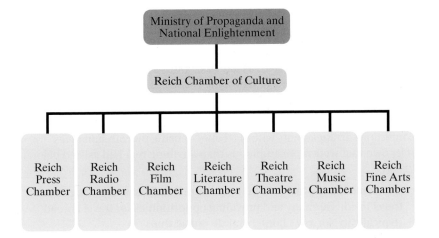

Goebbels was a shrewd propaganda operator. In his public statements he suggested that his goal was to integrate all 'national comrades' into a single 'national community' (*Volksgemeinschaft*) in which divisions of class and religion would be broken down. However, in practice he recognised that middle-aged and elderly people brought up within the working-class or Catholic camps were never going to be turned into committed Nazis. He therefore aimed at neutralising these sections of the population rather than converting them. The strategy he adopted involved deflecting people's attention away from politics by feeding them a diet of light entertainment.

Little of the output of the Reich Chamber of Film was overtly political. Half the films produced under Goebbels were romances or comedies and a quarter were thrillers. Only a small number could be described as crude National Socialist propaganda.

The same emphasis on depoliticising everyday life through popular entertainment can be seen in the output of the Reich Chamber of Radio: a lot of light music was played. The Nazis attached particular importance to the radio as a means of communication: in the 1930s the availability of the *Volksempfänger* ('People's Receiver') at low cost gave Germany the highest rate of radio ownership in the world.

Bear in mind, too, that working-class Germans are likely to have been influenced to some degree by Goebbels' efforts to build up a personality cult around Hitler. They may have been particularly impressed by claims that Hitler had masterminded victory in the 'battle for work' and was in the process of overthrowing the Versailles *Diktat*.

Essential notes

'National comrades' was the term that Nazis used to describe Germans who qualified for membership of the 'national community'. Non-Aryans (Jews, Roma and Sinti) were excluded from the 'national community'. So, too, were Aryans who suffered from mental illness or physical disability (because the Nazis deemed them 'genetically defective').

Essential notes

The extent to which the Nazis deserved credit for bringing down unemployment in Germany is open to question. The public works programme launched under the non-Nazi Economics Minister Schacht put some people back to work: so, too, did secret rearmament. But some historians argue that the world economic slump bottomed out in 1932 and was followed by 'natural' economic recovery.

☞ **Continued on the next two pages**

Leisure and cultural opportunities

Propaganda was not the only device the Nazis used to neutralise potential opposition. Also important was the KdF (*Kraft durch Freude*: 'Strength Through Joy') movement. The KdF was part of the German Labour Front, established by the Nazis in 1933 to replace the trades unions.

In part, the role of the KdF was to fill the gap left in working-class lives by the liquidation of the SPD and KPD. Before 1933 these parties had offered their followers a wide range of leisure and cultural opportunities (such as sports competitions, choirs and evening classes); after 1933 this sort of provision was made by the KdF.

The KdF did not confine itself to replacing Social Democratic or Communist arrangements with Nazi ones. It came up with initiatives of its own that were more ambitious than anything that had existed before 1933:

- It became heavily involved in the tourism business, sponsoring cheap travel inside Germany and providing opportunities for travel abroad (typically to Norway's fjords) on KdF cruise ships.

- In 1938 the KdF launched the *Volkswagen* ('People's Car') scheme. Would-be buyers were invited to pre-order their *Volkswagen* and to start paying 5 marks a week for it. 300 000 people signed up. No cars were ever delivered: the project was scrapped when war broke out.

The impact of propaganda and cultural provision

The Nazis certainly did not succeed in their stated objective of creating a single, cohesive 'national community'. But there is a lot of evidence that suggests that they secured a wide measure of acceptance of Nazi rule within the working-class and Catholic camps. Working-class Germans in particular seem to have appreciated the leisure opportunities made available to them through the KdF. No doubt they were similarly appreciative of the increased holiday entitlements they received in the Nazi era. The very poorest also benefited from 'Winter Aid', a Nazi-organised charitable enterprise.

Conclusion: dictatorship by consent?

The claim that 'the Third Reich was not a dictatorship maintained by force' (Götz Aly, *Hitler's Beneficiaries: Plunder, Racial Warfare and the Nazi Welfare State*, 2007) has not gone unchallenged. A prominent critic of the idea of 'dictatorship by consent' is the British historian Richard Evans:

Source 3
(From Richard Evans, *The Third Reich in Power*, published by Penguin 2005)

Some historians argue that the Nazis did not rule by terror at all, suggesting that after 1933 at least, terror was highly selective. The truth is that far from Nazi terror being levelled exclusively against small and despised minorities, the threat of arrest, prosecution and incarceration in increasingly brutal and violent conditions loomed over everyone in the Third Reich. The regime intimidated Germans into acquiescence, visiting a whole range of sanctions upon those who dared to oppose it. Yet terrorism was only one of the Third Reich's techniques of rule. For the Nazis did not just seek to batter the population into passive, sullen acquiescence. They wanted to rouse it into positive, enthusiastic endorsement of their ideals and their policies.

Evans supports his interpretation with a number of detailed arguments:

- He points out that Nazi terror in 1933 was not selective but involved a large-scale and ferocious onslaught on the Social Democratic and Communist Parties – parties that in the Weimar Republic's last free election (November 1932) between them won more than 13 million votes. He adds that Catholics did not emerge unscathed from the Nazi seizure of power either.

- He suggests that the fact that the number of concentration camp detainees in the 1930s was relatively small does not mean that the Nazis did not rely on terror. The mere existence of the *Gestapo* and the concentration camps, he maintains, created a climate of fear and acted as a warning to the population not to step out of line.

- He argues that it is a mistake to attach too much importance to the fact that the *Gestapo* was a comparatively small organisation. The Nazis, he notes, had several instruments of coercion at their disposal apart from the *Gestapo*:

  1. The regular courts dealt with political dissidents as well as the *Gestapo*. In 1932–7 Germany's prison population nearly doubled, with many of the increasing number of inmates having been sentenced for political offences.

  2. The local Nazi *Blockleiter* or 'block wardens' (200 000 of them) and organisations such as the Hitler Youth and Labour Front were part of the Nazi terror apparatus, keeping people under surveillance and reporting them to the *Gestapo*.

  3. In the professions and public services, people's jobs and livelihoods were at risk if they acquired a reputation for negativity towards the regime.

Finally, bear in mind the technical difficulties facing the historian studying popular opinion in Nazi Germany in the 1930s. There are no public opinion polls or election results to go on, and the sources that do exist – reports on the state of public opinion produced by the secret police and by the Social Democratic Party in exile (the SOPADE reports) – have to be treated with caution. In these circumstances certainty is difficult and the best the historian can do is weigh the balance of probabilities.

Examiners' notes

Richard Evans maintains that the criminal law, the regular courts and the state prison system – and not the *Gestapo* and the concentration camps – were the principal instruments of terror in the Third Reich. He argues that historians who focus their attention solely on the *Gestapo* and the concentration camps and ignore other, more important, forms of repression and control seriously under-estimate the extent to which terror was a feature in the lives of the great majority of ordinary Germans in the 1930s.

The Nazi state

You are required to have an understanding of the controversies surrounding the structure (or the structurelessness) and efficiency of the Nazi regime. This is a challenging topic. You need, as a starting point, to have a basic knowledge of the institutions and characteristics of the Nazi state:

Major institutions of the Nazi state, 1936 (the names given are those of government ministers and service chiefs who were not members of the Nazi Party – you do not need to learn them)

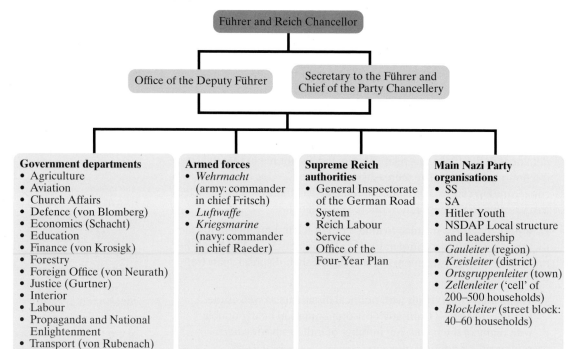

Führer and Reich Chancellor

Office of the Deputy Führer

Secretary to the Führer and Chief of the Party Chancellery

Government departments
- Agriculture
- Aviation
- Church Affairs
- Defence (von Blomberg)
- Economics (Schacht)
- Education
- Finance (von Krosigk)
- Forestry
- Foreign Office (von Neurath)
- Justice (Gurtner)
- Interior
- Labour
- Propaganda and National Enlightenment
- Transport (von Rubenach)

Armed forces
- *Wehrmacht* (army: commander in chief Fritsch)
- *Luftwaffe*
- *Kriegsmarine* (navy: commander in chief Raeder)

Supreme Reich authorities
- General Inspectorate of the German Road System
- Reich Labour Service
- Office of the Four-Year Plan

Main Nazi Party organisations
- SS
- SA
- Hitler Youth
- NSDAP Local structure and leadership
- *Gauleiter* (region)
- *Kreisleiter* (district)
- *Ortsgruppenleiter* (town)
- *Zellenleiter* ('cell' of 200–500 households)
- *Blockleiter* (street block: 40–60 households)

Essential notes

Number of times the Cabinet met each year before its abolition in 1938

1933	72
1934	19
1935	12
1936	4
1937	7

Characteristics of the Nazi state

The Nazis suspended the 1919 Constitution through the passage of the Reichstag Fire Decree and the Enabling Act but did not replace it with a new one. Weimar political institutions such as the Cabinet and the Reichstag survived into the Nazi era, though meetings were increasingly rare and served no real purpose. The Presidency existed as a separate institution until Hindenburg's death in 1934, whereupon Hitler merged the offices of President and Chancellor and styled himself 'Führer and Reich Chancellor'.

The Nazis retained all pre-1933 government departments, leaving a number of them, until the later 1930s, in the hands of non-Nazi conservatives who had first come into office in 1932 as members of von Papen's 'cabinet of barons'. In the early years of Nazi rule the government was thus technically a coalition. Four new government departments were created in 1933 (Aviation, Church Affairs, Education, and Propaganda and National Enlightenment) and one in 1934 (Forestry).

In addition to ordinary government departments, Hitler established three 'Supreme Reich Authorities': the General Inspectorate of the German Road System (1933), the Reich Labour Service (1934) and the Office of the Four-Year Plan (1936). The Supreme Reich Authorities were specialist agencies accountable only to Hitler. They could operate without reference to each other or to government departments and they had the power to issue decrees, enabling them, for example, to conscript individuals.

There was no clear line of division between state institutions and Nazi Party organisations. Himmler's SS, for example, was a party organisation, but by the mid-1930s the SS empire included state institutions, one of them being the *Gestapo*.

There was multiple office-holding (sometimes called 'administrative pluralism') at both national and local levels. Examples include Goebbels (Minister for Propaganda and *Gauleiter* of Berlin), Rust (Education Minister and *Gauleiter* of South Hanover-Braunschweig) and, at the local level, Adolf Wagner (simultaneously *Gauleiter* of Munich-Upper Bavaria and Reich Governor of Bavaria).

The army escaped *Gleichschaltung* in 1933 and until the late 1930s retained its autonomy.

Radicalisation, 1937–8

The Nazi regime was dynamic rather than static. An important turning point came 1937–8 when non-Nazi conservatives in the government expressed alarm about the pace of German rearmament and the army chiefs voiced concern about what they saw as Hitler's headlong rush towards war. Hitler responded by sweeping his critics aside and Nazifying his government further:

- In 1937 Economics Minister Schacht, a critic of high levels of military spending, resigned, leaving the Nazi Goering as Germany's economic supremo.

- The *Wehrmacht* was brought to heel in 1938. Blomberg (Defence Minister) and Fritsch (army commander in chief) were pressured into resigning after allegations of sexual misconduct were made against them. Sixteen other generals were retired and 44 more transferred to lesser commands. The Defence Ministry was abolished, allowing Hitler to exercise closer personal control over the army. He then put the army further in its place by allowing the SS to set up its own military units (the Waffen–SS), breaking a promise he had made to his generals in 1934 that no military force other than the *Wehrmacht* would be permitted in Germany.

- Foreign Minister Neurath was dismissed and replaced by the Nazi Joachim von Ribbentrop (1938).

Essential notes

The multiple office-holder who outdid all others was Goering. The positions he occupied in 1936 were:

- Director of Four-Year Plan
- Chief of Prussian *Gestapo*
- Aviation Minister
- Commander in chief of the *Luftwaffe*
- Reich Forestry Minister
- Reich Hunting Master
- President of the Reichstag.

Multiple office-holding was a source of inefficiency because the individuals who held a number of jobs became over-stretched.

Hitler's role in the Nazi state

Hitler's role and importance in the government of Nazi Germany have been the subject of extensive debate among historians. Some see the Third Reich as a monocratic, Hitler-centred, state in which the will of the Führer was decisive, while others see it as a polycratic state in which Hitler's voice was only one (albeit an important one) among many.

Nazi Germany as a 'monocratic' state

There are persuasive arguments that support the view that Hitler was the dominant figure in the Nazi state, the pivot around whom everything turned. The Nazi Party from the mid-1920s onwards was structured around the *Führerprinzip*. It was a 'leadership party' in which subordinates were expected to obey the commands of their superiors without question. In practice, there was at all levels of the party acceptance of the need for one all-powerful leader.

Hitler had no serious leadership rivals. Röhm and Gregor Strasser might be thought of as belonging to this category but they were eliminated on the 'Night of the Long Knives' in 1934. Hitler's chief lieutenants (Goering, Himmler and Goebbels) posed no sort of a threat to him: they viewed him with adulation.

Both in the 1930s and afterwards leading Nazis gave the impression that in the Third Reich the will of one man, and one man alone, was decisive. In 1936, for example, the leading Nazi lawyer Hans Frank declared: 'Our constitution is the will of the Führer.' Nazi defendants at the Nuremberg war crimes trials insisted that Hitler had been a dominant figure whose decisions could not be questioned (admittedly they had a vested interest for making this claim).

None of Hitler's subordinates ever imposed his will against the wishes of the Führer on a matter of importance.

Access to Hitler was essential to any Nazi potentate who hoped to flourish. Goebbels, Himmler and later Speer were among those who had a keen sense of the importance of proximity to the Führer and went out of their way to ensure they had regular face-to-face contact with him. Subordinates who were unable to break into Hitler's inner circle – Agriculture Minister Darré is an example – were the ones who lost out in the Third Reich's power struggles.

Source 4
(From Eberhard Jäckel, *Hitler's World View*, published by Wesleyan University 1969)

A complex administrative system on the one hand passed along to the Führer all matters requiring his decision, and on the other hand formulated and handed down the so-called Führer-decisions, which were frequently oral. This system was based on a concept of absolute obedience which comes closest to the concept of following orders as it prevails in the military, from where it was probably derived. Alone Hitler planned, alone he decided, alone he ruled.

Hitler's leadership style

Historians who question the idea of a Hitler-centred and Hitler-driven Nazi state point above all to Hitler's distinctive leadership style and its consequences:

- He did not work hard: he got up late (10am), had a long lunch, some afternoon appointments and then watched films in the evening.

- He rarely stayed in one place for long: he moved between Berlin (which he disliked), Munich and his house near Berchtesgaden in the Bavarian Alps.

- He disliked paperwork of any kind: he did not read documents prepared by officials or ministers and wrote virtually nothing himself.

- He refused to immerse himself in detail and left much to his subordinates.

- He tolerated, even welcomed, in-fighting and empire-building among his lieutenants. His attitude owed something to his belief that he should, as the nation's leader, remain above politics and not demean himself by taking sides in everyday political squabbles. Another factor was his Social Darwinist assumption that struggle was natural and inevitable. 'He lets things take their course until the stronger man has won the day,' said one of his *Gauleiters*.

- After the period of *Gleichschaltung* (1933–4) Hitler became increasingly detached from domestic politics in Germany. Foreign affairs held his attention on a sustained basis but he intervened only fitfully and haphazardly in domestic policy.

It was a result of Hitler's 'hands off' approach that powerful competing bureaucratic empires ('polycracy') arose.

'Working towards the Führer'

The view that the Nazi state was Hitler-driven may appear to be wholly incompatible with the idea that it was a jumble of competing power centres. However, an attempt to reconcile them has been made by the British historian Ian Kershaw. The key to understanding Hitler's role in the Nazi state, says Kershaw, is the concept of 'working towards the Führer'. It can be summarised as follows:

- As Führer, Hitler was the linchpin of the entire Nazi system and the only link between its component parts.

- Hitler's way of operating invited his subordinates to anticipate his wishes and to initiate things without his explicit prior approval.

- If subordinates correctly anticipated Hitler's wishes they were allowed to carry on undisturbed; if they did not, he intervened and stopped them.

- Hitler was therefore a dictator who did not have to dictate.

Essential notes

Some historians (Alan Bullock, for instance, in *Hitler: A Study in Tyranny*) have argued that Hitler deliberately pursued a policy of 'divide and rule'. However, given his unassailable political position, he had no real need of such a policy.

Essential notes

The phrase 'working towards the Führer' comes from a speech made by a senior Nazi official, Werner Willikens, in 1934:

'Everyone knows that the Führer can hardly dictate from above everything which he intends to realise sooner or later. Up till now everyone with a post in the new Germany has worked best when he has, so to speak, worked towards the Führer. Very often it has been the case that individuals have waited for orders and instructions. Unfortunately, the same will be true in the future. But it is the duty of everybody to try to work towards the Führer along the lines he would wish. Anyone who makes mistakes will notice it soon enough.'

(From William Stuckart, senior official in the interior ministry, 1941)

'This excessive fragmentation of agencies leads to war between offices, duplicated work, empty work, unproductive work, additional expense of administration and a bloated state machine.'

Inefficiency of the Nazi state

The Nazi state was chaotic and in some respects inefficient. The main form that such inefficiency took was duplication of effort and consequent waste of resources. The main reasons for inefficiency were empire-building, 'turf battles' and a lack of coordination.

Empire-building

Hitler's 'hands-off' approach to government left ambitious subordinates free to try to carve out personal fiefdoms.

The most successful empire-builder in Nazi Germany was Himmler. By 1936 he had won control of all policing in Germany. In the later 1930s he expanded into new areas, with the formation of the Waffen–SS and involvement in anti-Semitic policy. In 1941 he was given responsibility for the 'Final Solution'. By the latter stages of the war Himmler was presiding over a vast, sprawling empire that, apart from its role within Germany, effectively controlled much of Nazi-occupied Europe.

Empire-building contributed to inefficiency not only by giving rise to 'turf battles' between Nazi potentates but also by compelling them to devote a great deal of time to currying favour with Hitler.

Source 5
(From Joseph Bendersky, *A History of Nazi Germany,* published by Rowman & Littlefield 1956)

The Nazi new order was not a model of Germanic order and efficiency, with selfless party officials devoting their lives to the common interest or the goals of national socialism. Government in the Third Reich was characterised by jealousy and bureaucratic empire-building. Party officials more often than not tended to view the will of the Führer, the welfare of the nation, and the goals of the ideology from the perspective of their own career advancement, or the narrow interest of their particular organisation. Party officials engaged in bureaucratic wars to expand their power and the area controlled by their organisation at the expense of other party or state offices.

'Turf battles'

The history of the Third Reich is littered with 'turf battles' – struggles for control over particular areas of policy – between Hitler's subordinates. Three factors made such battles inevitable:

- the scale of the ambitions of Nazi bosses like Himmler, Goebbels and Goering
- Hitler's detachment from everyday politics
- the lack of any clearly defined and clearly understood division of responsibility between the various government and Nazi Party agencies.

The struggle for control of policing in Germany 1933–6 is a good example of a 'turf battle' because the main participants were all political heavyweights: Frick, the Interior Minister, a veteran Nazi who had been present at the Beer Hall *Putsch* in 1923, Himmler, head of the SS, and Goering, Hitler's deputy.

Essential notes

Another 'turf battle' was over control of economic policy. In 1936 Goering was made head of the Office of the Four-Year Plan with the task of making Germany economically self-sufficient. This put him on a collision course with Schacht, the Minister of Economics, and also the Ministers of Labour, Transport and Agriculture. This time it was Goering who won the day.

In 1933 Frick, as Interior Minister, had overall responsibility for all German police forces. The power-hungry Himmler controlled the Nazi Party's in-house security police, the SD, and in 1933 was given control of the police in Bavaria. Goering was involved in policing as Prussia's Interior Minister: in 1933 he formed the *Gestapo* out of the political branch of the Prussian police. After three years' relentless intriguing Himmler saw off his rivals. In 1936 Hitler appointed him Chief of German Police.

> **Source 6**
> (From Ian Kershaw, *Hitler, the Germans and the Final Solution*, published by Yale University Press 2008)
>
> Hitler was on the whole a non-interventionist dictator as far as government administration was concerned. His sporadic directives when they came, tended to be unclear and to be conveyed verbally, usually by Lammers, the head of the Reich Chancellery. Hitler chaired no formal committees after the first years of the regime, when the Cabinet (which he hated chairing) faded into non-existence.

Absence of coordination

Hitler's 'hands-off' approach encouraged subordinates to act on their own initiative. But no machinery was established that ensured that the work of different parts of the government machine was properly coordinated:

- Hitler showed no inclination to coordinate policy himself.

- Under the Nazis the Cabinet withered away.

- This left Hans Lammers, Head of the Reich Chancellery, as the only coordinating link between Hitler and the heads of government agencies. Lammers was influential but he was not a heavy political hitter able to take on Nazi chieftains such as Himmler on equal terms. His main task was to supervise the making of new laws by circulating proposals prepared by one department, to other departments for their approval. In the event of disagreement Lammers was sometimes able to mediate between departments but he could not override them.

Assessment

The Nazi state was not a well-oiled, smoothly functioning machine. Do not, however, assume too readily that because it was polycratic and anarchic it was necessarily hopelessly inefficient.

People mattered, as well as organisational structures. There were some in the Nazi hierarchy who were lazy and corrupt but many others who were industrious and resourceful servants of the regime and its ideology.

The Supreme Reich Authorities were, in general, effective bodies. This is especially true of Todt's Roads Inspectorate, where Todt's administrative apparatus 'enabled his goals to be realised with maximum efficiency and speed' (Michael Freeman, *Atlas of Nazi Germany*, 1987).

In the 1930s the Nazi regime ran elaborate propaganda and internal security operations and built up a formidable military machine: in some respects the Nazi regime was all too efficient.

Essential notes

Before 1933 the Cabinet was the key coordinating body.

Examiners' notes

Hitler habitually put off making decisions but when he decided to act he could move swiftly and ruthlessly – and the polycratic nature of the state was no obstacle to him doing so. Examples of swift and ruthless action are the 'Night of the Long Knives' (1934) and the Blomberg–Fritsch affair (1938).

Examiners' notes

In Section B you will need to weigh the claims made by the sources and integrate your own knowledge before reaching a judgement. For example, how far are the ways noted here in which the regime was efficient outweighed by the ways in which it was inefficient, indicated in Sources 5 and 6?

Perspectives of the Nazi state

In 1939 the American historian Carlton Hayes described Germany as a totalitarian dictatorship in which the will of the dictator was imposed on society through a highly disciplined Nazi Party. It was in reaction to his kind of leader-centred, top-down interpretation of the Third Reich that historians in the 1960s and 1970s began to look at Nazi Germany from the bottom up – that is, to explore the structures of government and society in Germany in the Nazi era.

Structuralists and intentionalists

Essential notes

Martin Broszat's *The Hitler State* is a pioneering and classic examination of the internal structure of the Nazi regime.

Source 7
(From Martin Broszat, *The Hitler State*, published by Longman 1981)

My work offers a corrective to the over-simplified picture of a monolithic system and of a well-oiled super-state which derived from the concept of totalitarianism. Hitler practised no direct and systematic leadership but from time to time jolted the government or the Party into action, supported one or other initiative of Party functionaries or departmental heads and thwarted others, ignored them or left them to carry on without a decision. Thus in all those areas of policy with which Hitler never or seldom bothered, the absolute supremacy of the Führer spawned a growing system of rival power centres, all trying to put forward schemes in the name of Hitler, all trying to get access to him and to get 'Führer commands' to back them up.

There has been a general reaction against the application of structural history to the Nazi regime. This is particularly true of many of the new products of the Hitler literature which give the impression that the personal will of Adolf Hitler himself solely or primarily determined the history of the Third Reich. That is all the more reason to react to the growing tendency of historians to resort to the history of personalities.

Examiners' notes

In your analysis of Section B sources you need to be able to cross-reference – that is, to explain the relationship between the interpretation offered in one source and those offered in others. For example, the interpretation of government in the Third Reich offered in Source 7 would clearly challenge a source that described the Nazi state as highly organised and efficiently run. The question of whether the interpretation offered in Source 7 is well-founded is a matter you would have to address on the basis of your own knowledge of (for example) Hitler's leadership style and developments in key areas such as the management of the economy and racial policy.

'Structuralist' accounts of the Nazi state may have undermined earlier 'totalitarian' interpretations of it as a 'well-oiled machine' but they came under strong criticism themselves. Critics of the 'structuralist' approach argue that depictions of a semi-detached Führer, loosely presiding over a jungle of competing political empires, mistakenly displaces Hitler from the centre of the Third Reich. Historians who emphasise the centrality of Hitler's personality, ideas and intentions in the functioning of the Nazi state are commonly referred to as 'intentionalists'.

Source 8
(From Lucy S. Dawidowicz, *The War against the Jews 1933–45*, published by Holt, Rinehart and Winston 1975)

To be sure, some Nazis in high places ran their jurisdictions like personal fiefdoms, but none ever shared power with Hitler or governed independently as a 'polycrat'. In areas where Hitler failed clearly to articulate his wishes, his underlings vied with each other in trying to carry out the policies that they thought most satisfactorily reflected his wishes. None dared carry out a policy that did not accord with Hitler's will.

In repudiating what he called 'the growing tendency of historians to resort to the history of personalities', Broszat downgraded Hitler's role in the dictatorship. This structuralist interpretation fails to convince because it takes no account of ideas and intentions, even such monstrous ones as Hitler's. For history begins in the minds of men and women, in the ideas they hold and in the decisions they take.

Agreement and disagreement

Making sense of the debate between 'structuralist' and 'intentionalist' historians is no easy matter. There are points on which they are agreed and matters about which they strongly disagree. You need to be able to pinpoint both.

Points of agreement between 'structuralist' and 'intentionalist' historians can be summarised as follows:

- Both accept that the Nazi state contained political fiefdoms, or empires, such as those headed by Himmler, Goebbels and Goering.

- Both recognise that Hitler often failed to communicate his intentions clearly and explicitly to his subordinates.

- Both accept that the Nazi state was chaotic, disorderly and in many respects inefficient.

The key differences between structuralists and intentionalists lie in their interpretation of Hitler's role in the Third Reich and in their underlying assumptions about the process of historical change. Their differing views of the Nazi state owe a great deal to these differing underlying assumptions (which are illustrated by Sources 7 and 8).

Examiners' notes

Source 8 highlights one of the key issues you need to consider if you are to be able to comment effectively on whether or not Hitler was the central, dominating, all-powerful figure in the Nazi state: were Hitler's decisions ever ignored or altered by his subordinates?

There are two other questions that you might consider:

1. Was Hitler ever unwilling or reluctant to make decisions because he feared that he would run into serious opposition from his subordinates?

2. Is there any evidence at all which suggests that Hitler was the prisoner of powerful social forces (the army, say, or big business) that he dared not offend?

If the answer to all three questions mentioned here is 'yes', it would be difficult to see Hitler as an all-powerful figure in the Nazi state.

Structuralists and intentionalists

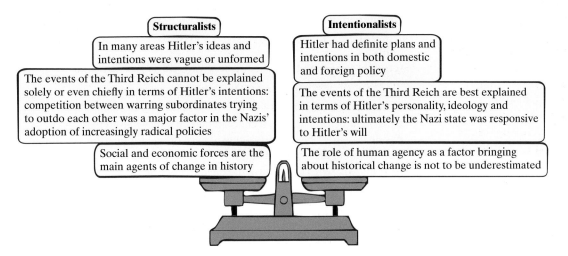

Structuralists

In many areas Hitler's ideas and intentions were vague or unformed

The events of the Third Reich cannot be explained solely or even chiefly in terms of Hitler's intentions: competition between warring subordinates trying to outdo each other was a major factor in the Nazis' adoption of increasingly radical policies

Social and economic forces are the main agents of change in history

Intentionalists

Hitler had definite plans and intentions in both domestic and foreign policy

The events of the Third Reich are best explained in terms of Hitler's personality, ideology and intentions: ultimately the Nazi state was responsive to Hitler's will

The role of human agency as a factor bringing about historical change is not to be underestimated

Essential notes

Seen from the German point of view, the war of 1939–45 can be broken down into three phases:

- a period of conquest, 1939–42
- a period of decisive reverses, 1942–3, which included defeats at Stalingrad (August 1942–January 1943) and Kursk (July 1943) on the Eastern Front and El Alamein (October 1942) in North Africa
- a period of retreat, 1943–5, key points of which were the entry of the Red Army into Poland (mid-1944), then Germany itself (January 1945) and the Allied landings in Normandy (July 1944).

Hitler committed suicide on 30 April 1945.

Life in wartime Germany: morale, opposition, resistance

Hitler was convinced that Germany's armies in the First World War had been defeated by the collapse of the home front. He was determined to ensure that history did not repeat itself. The result in the early stages of the war was 'a reluctance to ask the public to bear sacrifices' (Gordon Craig, *Germany 1866–1945*, 1978):

- Food rationing was introduced in 1939 but allowances to begin with were fairly generous.
- The leisure and entertainment provided by the KdF continued.
- Hitler was unwilling to see the mobilisation of Germany's resources extend as far as conscripting women into the industrial workforce: he still saw the primary role of women as bearing children for the Reich.

There was no great enthusiasm for war in Germany in 1939. One historian (Helmut Krausnick) has described the public mood on the outbreak of war as one of 'reluctant loyalty'. However, the regime's relatively limited demands on the civilian population, plus a string of morale-boosting military victories, meant that it had little to fear on the home front during the first two years of the war.

Reasons for deteriorating civilian morale, 1942–5

In the middle and later years of the war, attitudes within the civilian population towards the regime and the war changed. For a variety of reasons, morale deteriorated sharply.

Military defeat

- German civilians knew in 1942–5 how badly things were going at the battle front: defeats on the scale of Stalingrad (1943) and Kursk (1943) were too big to be covered up.
- Fighting on the retreat meant increased casualties. The death toll in the latter stages of the war was much higher than it was in the period of conquest. Nearly two-thirds of all German servicemen killed in the 1939–45 war (one estimate suggests a figure of just over 5 million) died in 1944–5. In this period the lives of many civilians were shattered by bereavement.

> **Source 1**
> (From Lizzie Collingham, *The Taste of War: World War Two and the Battle for Food*, published by Allen Lane 2011)
>
> In the city of Cologne, the last two years of the war were appalling. Lengthening food queues were matched by long walks to work as the public transport system broke down. Lack of fuel for heating, combined with frequent air raids, made home life debilitating, and the shabby clothing and worn shoes gave the civilian population a depressing air. There were no work shoes to be had or rubber boots. Washing was difficult with the tiny piece of inferior soap that was allocated on the monthly ration. The deaths of friends and neighbours from the bombing campaign, and the increasing loss of men at the front to death and injury all wore down civilian morale.

Dislocation and disruption

- Retreat also meant large numbers of evacuees and refugees. Large numbers of children were evacuated to rural areas as the Allied air offensive intensified from 1943 onwards. In 1945, 5 million civilians living in the eastern parts of Germany became refugees, fleeing westwards to escape the oncoming Red Army.

- Lives were further disrupted by the Nazi regime's desperate attempts to overcome labour shortages. In 1944 a compulsory 60-hour work week was introduced and holidays were banned.

Shortages and hardship

- Rationing became increasingly severe. In 1942, bread and meat allowances were cut drastically. Food and fuel became increasingly scarce in Germany as the war went on.

- Shortages depressed the morale of the entire civilian population, but mothers worried about how to feed their families were perhaps worst affected.

The impact of bombing

Between 1943 and 1945 German cities came under intense attack from the air. The USAF bombed by day, the RAF by night. One of the aims of the strategic bombing offensive was to inflict damage on the German economy, but it was also designed to break civilian morale. In the face of this onslaught the German people displayed considerable resilience, but it nevertheless left them traumatised and exhausted. Bombing was probably the most important cause of deteriorating morale, 1942–5.

Statistics relating to the Anglo–American strategic bombing offensive

Tonnage of bombs dropped by RAF and USAF, 1939–45	2.7 million
German civilians killed	300 000
German civilians injured	780 000
Homes destroyed	2 million
Number of Germans homeless, 1945	7 million

Propaganda and terror in wartime

Deteriorating morale had tangible consequences. Perhaps the most alarming, from the regime's point of view, was large-scale absenteeism from work, which had knock-on effects on industrial production.

In peacetime the Nazi regime had relied on a combination of propaganda and terror to secure obedience. These were also the weapons it used in wartime. Goebbels and Himmler were the key figures in the regime's attempts to combat the damaging effects of declining morale in the later stages of the war.

Essential notes

One way in which low morale expressed itself was absenteeism from work. It undermined the war effort and, from the point of view of the Nazi authorities, was not easy to combat.

Essential notes

Absenteeism from work had serious effects in later years of the war. Morale affected the war effort.

☞ Continued on the next two pages

Essential notes

In the later stages of the war Goebbels, appointed Reich Commissioner for Total War in 1944, became the public face of the Nazi regime in Germany. He criss-crossed the country, visiting bombed cities and urging people to fight on. Hitler, by contrast, more or less completely disappeared from public view, spending his time at the 'Wolf's Lair', his military headquarters in East Prussia, and later at his bunker in Berlin.

Goebbels and wartime propaganda

Goebbels threw himself into the task of rallying public opinion behind the war effort with immense energy. In 1943 he called upon the German people to wage 'total war'. He warned of the horrors that would follow a Soviet invasion and he claimed that Germany was devising miracle weapons that would enable it to snatch victory from the jaws of defeat.

Goebbels' propaganda offensive, however, failed to halt the decline in morale. By 1944–5 Nazi propaganda simply lacked credibility:

- The inflated, boastful propaganda claims made in the period of conquest were shown to be hollow.
- The 'Hitler myth' largely collapsed: it became difficult in the later stages of the war to see Hitler as a miracle-worker.
- Rightly or wrongly, working-class Germans believed that the wealthier classes were largely unaffected by rationing and wartime shortages: in these circumstances the Nazis talk of a classless *Volksgemeinschaft* also appeared hollow.

Himmler and terror

Himmler's power in the Third Reich reached its zenith in the war years. Apart from presiding over his growing SS empire, he was appointed Minister of the Interior in 1943. Obedience and consent among the civilian population in the later stages of the war owed more to Himmler's regime of terror than to Goebbels' propaganda.

The regime used a variety of methods to keep the civilian population under control in wartime:

- A range of new criminal offences was created, for example, undermining the war effort, listening to foreign radio stations and hoarding food.
- The ordinary courts were pressured by the regime to impose harsh sentences on offenders. The number of death sentences imposed by the ordinary courts rose from 139 in 1939 to over 4000 in 1944. The prison population also rose sharply. If the courts imposed sentences that the SS deemed too lenient it simply intervened in the legal process and increased them.
- The numbers detained in the concentration camp system within Germany (not to be confused with the extermination camps in Poland) increased from 25 000 in 1919 to over 700 000 in 1945. Large numbers of wartime concentration camp inmates were foreigners from occupied Europe, but many were German. Thousands of Germans, for example, were arrested after the attempt on Hitler's life in 1944.

Opposition and resistance

Everyday dissent and nonconformity became increasingly common towards the end of the war. Typical forms included:

- listening to foreign radio stations such as the BBC
- refusing to give the 'Heil Hitler!' salute
- buying or bartering food on the 'black market'

- telling anti-regime jokes
- failing to participate in the activities of Nazi organisations such as the Hitler Youth.

These are sometimes described as acts of 'minor' dissent, but remember that in circumstances where the Nazi regime was increasingly desperate they were high-risk activities.

There was also more resistance to Nazism in wartime than before 1939. Organised communist and Social Democrat resistance activity continued into the war years. The highest-profile wartime resistance groups were, however, middle and upper class in origin.

Wartime resistance groups

The 'White Rose' Group	The 'Kreisau Circle'	The 'Beck–Goerdeler' Group
Based at Munich University, it consisted of idealistic middle-class students, all devout Christians, who were horrified by Nazi anti-Jewish excesses. Its members distributed anti-Nazi leaflets and daubed the walls of public buildings with anti-Nazi graffiti. Its leading figures, Hans and Sophie Scholl, Christoph Probst, Kurt Huber, Willi Graf and Alexander Schmorell, were arrested in 1943 and beheaded.	Named after the country estate of one of its leaders, the 'Kreisau Circle' was a loose association of upper-class intellectuals and political moderates brought together by a shared loathing of Nazi barbarism. It was essentially a discussion group that focused on planning a post-war democratic Germany, but some of its leading figures (Helmuth von Moltke, Adam von Trott du Solz, Peter Graf Yorck von Wartenburg) made contact with the Beck–Goerdeler group and paid the price (arrest and execution).	A group of old-fashioned upper-class conservative nationalists, several of whom had been favourably disposed towards Nazism in the 1930s but turned against Hitler when it became clear he was leading Germany to disaster. Their plan was to remove Hitler from power by assassinating him. Goerdeler was a government official in the early years of Nazi rule and Beck was, until 1938, a senior army general. Beck committed suicide after the 1944 'July Plot'. Goerdeler was executed.

How seriously did wartime resistance threaten the Nazi regime?

- Left-wing resistance in the war years did not pose a substantial threat to the regime: SPD and communist underground networks had largely been destroyed by the *Gestapo* in the 1930s.

- Middle- and upper-class resistance groups had different aims and motives and there were few links between them.

- At no stage in the war was there any sign of mass protest or a 'revolution from below', which might have toppled the regime. This was in large part the result of SS terror, but there were other factors too: bombing focused people's attention on day-to-day survival and diverted it away from politics and, because the Allies clearly had no interest in any sort of compromise peace, there appeared to be no alternative to fighting on.

- The military–conservative resistance nevertheless posed a serious threat to the regime because it had the capacity to get close enough to Hitler to assassinate him.

Essential notes

'Operation Valkyrie' was the name given to the military-conservative Beck–Goerdeler group's plan to kill Hitler and then to seize power in an army-led coup. One of the group, Colonel Claus von Stauffenberg, was a senior military planner whose work brought him into direct contact with Hitler. On 20 July he planted a bomb in a conference room at Hitler's 'Wolf's Lair' headquarters. It exploded, killing four people, Hitler not among them. This incident is often referred to as the 'July Plot'.

Examiners' notes

The issue of wartime resistance could be the subject of a question on life in wartime Germany. Be careful to note the exact focus of the question you are asked. There is a difference between simple resistance to the regime and resistance that threatens the regime. Take care to define what types of resistance you are assessing. For example, as well as active resistance, you might consider absence from essential work (see pages 86–7) to indicate resistance to the regime, but you will need to make clear the basis of your argument. Only a tiny minority of Germans were involved in active resistance.

Examiners' notes

You must be able to assess the efficiency of war production. Be sure that you have clear criteria in mind against which to make your assessment and that you can deploy precise evidence to support the points you make. For example, one criterion you might use is the extent to which the mismatches between spending and production identified in 1939 were reduced by better administration.

Essential notes

Fritz Todt was a Nazi civil engineer who, in the 1930s, acquired a reputation for getting things done. As head of the Roads Inspectorate he presided over the building of nearly 2000 miles [3200 km] of motorways, 1933–9. In 1938 his construction group, Organisation Todt, was given the task of building the West Wall, a line of bunkers and anti-tank barriers that ran the length of Germany's borders with Holland, Belgium and France.

The German war economy

Germany's preparations for war in the 1930s

German rearmament began in secret in 1933 and continued openly after 1935.

Hitler was anxious to ensure that Nazi Germany would have the ability to withstand an enemy blockade of the kind that had done so much damage in the 1914–18 war. The core aim of the Four-Year Plan, launched in 1936, was to make Germany as economically self-sufficient as possible. The results of the Plan were mixed:

- By 1939 Germany had an army of 3.8 million men and an air force of 3000 warplanes.
- In 1939 spending on armaments accounted for 23 per cent of Germany's gross national product compared with only 1 per cent in 1933.

Germany's readiness for war in 1939

Levels of munitions production in the late 1930s were disappointingly low despite heavy spending. When Germany attacked Poland in 1939, army chiefs were worried about shortages of ammunition. There were a number of reasons for this mismatch between spending and production: different agencies competed against each other for resources, production bottlenecks occurred in armaments factories as a result of labour shortages, some of the smaller armaments contractors were not geared up for mass production and the army insisted on quality of weaponry at the expense of quantity.

There were also worries among army chiefs in 1939 about Germany's capacity to fight a long war against several enemies. Of particular concern was the lack of guaranteed supplies of essential raw materials, especially oil.

Todt

The munitions shortages of 1939–40 led to Fritz Todt's appointment as Armaments Minister with responsibility for coordinating munitions production. He had some success in overcoming production bottlenecks, but was dragged into 'turf wars' with Goering's Office of the Four-Year Plan and the *Wehrmacht* (army), both of them unwilling to hand over their roles in the sphere of armaments production to Todt.

Speer

In 1942, following Todt's death in an air crash, Albert Speer took over as Armaments Minister.

Speer recognised that the era of quick German victories won by 'lightning war' (*Blitzkrieg*) methods was over and saw that Germany had to reorganise itself for a prolonged 'total war' against enemies (Britain, the Soviet Union and the USA) whose combined productive capacity far outweighed Germany's.

Germany did have some plus points in what was, nevertheless, clearly an unequal economic contest:

- It gained access to new food supplies and some key raw materials as a result of its conquests (French coal and iron ore, Rumanian oil, Ukrainian arable land).

- It captured large quantities of military equipment from countries it defeated, which it was able to convert for its own use.

- Most importantly, conquered territories provided Germany with much-needed supplies of labour. The Nazis put French and Russian prisoners of war to work in their factories and transported millions of civilians to Germany from Poland, France and other occupied territories to work as slave labourers. By 1944 there were 8 million slave labourers working in Germany – nearly one-fifth of the total work force.

Under Speer's direction big increases took place in armaments production. Between 1942 and 1944 weapon production tripled. Speer replaced a chaotic polycratic system (in which departments and agencies competed against each other for resources) with more orderly arrangements, including, for the first time, a proper central coordinating body ('Central Planning'):

- he concentrated production in a small number of gigantic factories

- he streamlined production by cutting out waste and duplication

- he sacked ineffective managers.

Speer's achievements were striking, not least because he had to contend with the effects of the Anglo–American strategic bombing offensive. As a result of his efforts, the war went on for longer than it might have done otherwise. But he could not prevent defeat.

Strengths and weaknesses of the German war economy

Essential notes

At first sight Speer was an unlikely choice as Todt's replacement. He was Hitler's architect and one of the Führer's personal favourites. He had no military connections and no experience working in heavy industry. He was, however, a supremely gifted organiser.

The management of the German economy under Speer

Central planning
An inner economic cabinet that oversaw the whole of the economy.

↓

Main committees
Supervised production of particular classes of equipment – tanks, aircraft, radio and so on

↓

Special committees
Responsible for the production of one type of aircraft or tank

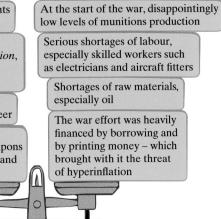

Strengths

Striking increases in armaments production in 1942–4

Economy displayed 'awful resilience' (Adam Tooze, *The Wages of Destruction*, 2006) in face of the Allied strategic bombing offensive

Belatedly, the economy was effectively organised under Speer

Germany produced a stream of high-quality, technologically advanced weapons – the *Panther* and Tiger tanks, the V1 and V2 rockets, the Me 262 jet-fighter

Weaknesses

At the start of the war, disappointingly low levels of munitions production

Serious shortages of labour, especially skilled workers such as electricians and aircraft fitters

Shortages of raw materials, especially oil

The war effort was heavily financed by borrowing and by printing money – which brought with it the threat of hyperinflation

Hitler's views were expressed in a 'letter on the Jewish question' in 1919:

> Jewry is clearly a racial and not a religious group. All that which is for other men a source of higher life – be it religion, socialism or democracy – is for the Jew merely a means to an end, namely, the satisfaction of his lust for power and money…

Examiners' notes

You will not be asked in Section A to answer questions about the period 1933–9, but you will need to be able to analyse the 'evolution of the Final Solution'. The material is included here to illustrate that the Nazi regime had no agreed anti-Jewish policy in 1939. You could, if relevant, make the same point in an essay, but do not get drawn into a description of events pre-1939.

Essential notes

Autarky is the technical term for economic self-sufficiency.

The Nazi Holocaust

Nazi anti-Semitism

The Nazis' 'all-devouring manic obsession with the Jews' (Ian Kershaw, *Hitler 1889–1936: Hubris*, 1998) was based on a number of assumptions:

- Jews were a race – a biologically distinct group – rather than a religious group.

- As a non-Aryan race, Jews could never be part of the German nation or *Volk*.

- Jews were Aryans' rivals in a Darwinist struggle for racial survival.

- Jews possessed a number of characteristics that made them exceptionally deadly rivals. They were megalomaniac, aiming at world domination; they were cohesive, their allegiance to each other transcending any loyalty they felt to the country in which they happened to live; and they were devious, hiding behind various stooges and accomplices such as the communists (Hitler was convinced that Russian communism was controlled by Jews).

Nazi persecution of Germany's Jews, 1933–9

Nazi persecution of Germany's half-million strong Jewish community was vicious but also fitful and erratic.

There were three waves of persecution – 1933, 1935 and 1938 – with a period of relative calm between them. Each wave of persecution followed a similar pattern: an outburst of violence and thuggery, in which the SA took the lead, followed by a round of anti-Semitic legislation. The outbursts of violence in 1933 and 1935 were spontaneous. In 1938 the violence was orchestrated – not by the regime as a whole but by Goebbels, anxious to ingratiate himself with Hitler after a period in which he had been out of favour.

On the eve of war in 1939 the Nazi regime had no agreed and settled anti-Jewish policy. There were competing policies. Goering, responsible for the Four-Year Plan, was committed to 'Aryanisation' (the confiscation and sale of Jewish property, with the proceeds being invested in the drive towards autarky) while Himmler was pushing for a policy of forced emigration that would make Germany *Judenfrei* (free of Jews).

The changing context of Nazi anti-Jewish policy, 1939–42

The context of Nazi anti-Jewish policy changed in 1939–42, principally as a result of German expansion and conquest:

- Poland, invaded by Germany in 1939, was home to 3 million Jews, one-third of the European total.

- The German invasions of France, Holland and Belgium (1940) and of Greece and Yugoslavia (1941), together with the alliances it formed with Rumania and Hungary (1941), left 2 million Jews living in west and south-east Europe, at the Nazis' mercy.

- Western Russia, attacked and largely occupied by Germany in 1941, contained 2.5 million Jews.

The chronology and geography of German expansion between 1939–42 need to be borne in mind if the complexities of Nazi racial policy in occupied Europe in these years are to be understood: Poland, Russia and the remainder of Europe were separate spheres of activity within which different things were done.

Bear in mind, too, that in occupied Poland and Russia the Nazis were able to operate out of public view. In Germany in the 1930s their actions had been observable by foreign diplomats. Under the cloak of secrecy Nazi racial policy became more radical.

Mass murder to genocide, 1939–42

There was no final, top-level Nazi decision in favour of a policy of systematic genocide until the latter part of 1941. As late as 1940 the Nazis were toying with a scheme to solve 'the Jewish problem' by forcing European Jews to migrate to the French colony of Madagascar. The German invasions of Poland and Russia, however, were accompanied by mass executions of Jews, mostly ordered by local SS commanders who were 'working towards the Führer'.

Poland, 1939–42

In September 1939 *Einsatzgruppen* SS followed the German armies into Poland. Their main task was to murder potential resistance leaders – army officers, landowners, intellectuals – many of whom were Jews. However, they were also responsible for numerous anti-Semitic atrocities that had nothing to do with neutralising opposition.

Defeated Poland was divided and dismantled. Eastern Poland went to Soviet Russia under the terms of the Nazi–Soviet Non-Aggression Pact. Three provinces in German-occupied Poland (Danzig–West Prussia, Upper Silesia and the Warthegau) were incorporated into the German Reich. The remainder was put under Nazi occupation and became an administrative area known as the General Government. Its Governor-General was Hans Frank.

The SS in 1939 hoped to deport German Jews to the General Government, but Frank opposed the scheme, claiming that he did not want to administer 'a refuse tip'.

From late 1939 onwards Poland's Jews were herded into ghettoes as an interim measure while the Nazis pondered their ultimate fate. Frank presided over this exercise. The biggest ghettoes were at Lodz, Warsaw and Krakow. Half a million Jews died in Poland's ghettoes as a result of malnutrition and disease.

Essential notes

The *Einsatzgruppen* (task forces) were part of Himmler's SS. Each *Einsatzgruppe* consisted of between 600 and 1000 men and was divided into four sub-units called *Einsatzkommando*. Members of *Einsatzgruppen* were drawn from different branches of the SS. Most were soldiers from the Waffen–SS, but others came from the *Gestapo* and SD.

Essential notes

A ghetto is part of a town or city inhabited by people of the same ethnic group, religion or social class. Ghettoes can result from poverty or disadvantage, but Nazi ghettoes were obviously created by design.

☞ **Continued on the next two pages**

Essential notes

Note that the pace of the genocide which took place in Poland was influenced by the economic difficulties Germany faced in 1942. During 1941–2 millions of foreigners were brought to Germany to work as slave labourers. These workers had to be fed if they were to be capable of productive work. One way in which the necessary food was made available from the Third Reich's limited supplies was by reducing the rations of the civilian population in countries under German occupation. Another was by killing Jews in Poland so that they did not need to be fed.

Essential notes

The biggest single atrocity carried out by an *Einsatzgruppe* took place at Babi Yar, a ravine outside the Ukrainian city of Kiev, in September 1941. Over a two-day period 33 000 Jews were murdered.

Examiners' notes

A key issue to examine is how far the Nazi Holocaust was planned.

By mid-1941 racial policy in the General Government was firmly in the hands of the SS. Frank had been marginalised. On Himmler's instructions, in autumn 1941 SS bosses began 'Operation Reinhard' – the building of extermination camps to which the surviving inhabitants of Poland's Jewish ghettoes would be sent. The first camp, at Chelmno, was opened in December 1941; Belzec, Sobibor and Treblinka followed over the next few months.

Poland and the Holocaust

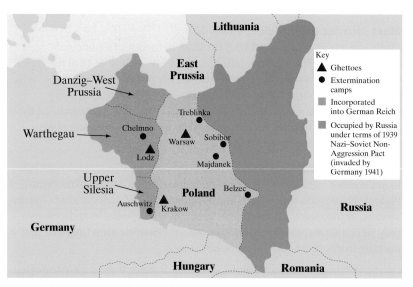

Russia, 1941–2

Operation Barbarossa, the German attack on Soviet Russia, was launched in June 1941. As in Poland, the invading German armies were followed by *Einsatzgruppen*. In Russia, however, the *Einsatzgruppen* targeted Jews – women and children as well as men – more explicitly than they had in Poland. *Einsatzgruppen* atrocities in Russia were also on a different scale from anything seen in Poland. In the period between June 1941 and April 1942 they butchered more than half a million Russian Jews by shooting or through the use of mobile gas wagons.

Ghettoisation differed in Russia, too. Jews in Poland were left in ghettoes for a prolonged period, whereas ghettoes in Russia were temporary holding centres in which people were kept only for days before execution.

Genocide

There is no written directive by Hitler ordering genocide. This is unsurprising: written orders were not the way that Hitler did business.

There is, however, circumstantial evidence that suggests that a green light for genocide was given at some point in the summer or autumn of 1941:

- In July 1941 Goering gave Heydrich, Himmler's deputy, an order to draft a plan for 'a total solution of the Jewish question'. Note that a 'total' solution in this context means one involving not only Jews in Poland and Russia but those in other parts of Nazi-occupied Europe as well.

- Interviewed at Nuremburg in 1946, Rudolf Höss, the first commandant of Auschwitz, maintained that Himmler had told him in mid-1941: 'The Führer has ordered the final solution of the Jewish problem and we, the SS, are to implement that order.'

- Adolf Eichmann, one of Heydrich's senior aides, claimed after the war that he had been told by his boss in autumn 1941 that: 'The Führer has ordered the physical destruction of the Jews.'

- The idea of using poison gas for mass killing is known to have been under discussion within the Nazi hierarchy in late 1941.

The notorious Wannsee Conference (January 1942) took place as a consequence of the green light for genocide having been given. At Wannsee, Heydrich informed 14 senior Nazi officials that the 'final solution' was to be the responsibility of the SS and would, in the first instance, involve the deportation of European Jews to Poland. The meeting then focused on points of detail, such as the definition of a Jew for the purposes of deportation.

After the Wannsee Conference the process of rounding up Jews across Nazi-occupied Europe got under way. Most European Jews were killed at the extermination camps at Auschwitz and Majdanek, though some were taken to the 'Operation Reinhard' camps set up to murder Poland's Jews. Auschwitz was the largest extermination site of the Holocaust: a million people died there in 1942–4.

Bear in mind that nearly half of the Holocaust's victims did not die in extermination camps, but in Poland's ghettoes, in Russia at the hands of the *Einsatzgruppen* or in the 'death marches' of 1944–5. When the Red Army entered Poland the Nazis emptied the extermination camps and forced surviving inmates to walk long distances, without food, proper clothing or shelter, to railway stations for transportation back into Germany.

The fate of Jewish Holocaust victims (millions)

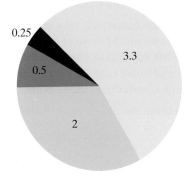

- Died in extermination camps
- Murdered by *Einsatzgruppen* in Russia
- Died of disease or malnutrition in Polish ghettoes
- Died in 1945 'death marches'

Essential notes

Decision-making in relation to the Holocaust after 1939 was no different from decision-making in other areas of policy in Nazi Germany:

- Hitler gave his subordinates verbal indications of his views but not direct written instructions.

- His subordinates in the 'wild East' (Poland and Russia) did not take initiatives that they knew to be at odds with Hitler's wishes – they acted in ways they hoped would meet with his approval. Those exercising power in Poland and Russia in the early 1940s assumed (correctly) that in no circumstances were they going to find themselves condemned by Hitler for being excessively harsh and brutal.

- When there were clashes between subordinates (for example, between Frank and Himmler in 1939–41 for power in the area of the General Government), Hitler awaited the outcome and then gave his approval to the strongest competitor.

- In the end nothing was done in Poland or Russia after 1939 that did not have Hitler's approval.

Introduction

This section of the book covers the skills you must use to gain a high mark.

Your Unit 3 exam will comprise of two parts: Section A and Section B. The Section A questions are essay questions, while the Section B questions are source-based. While you do need to have learned and understood the subject content, you won't get many marks for simply repeating what you know. Each question will always have a specific focus and you need to be able to: identify this, select the best evidence to use and then apply it in a suitable way. The guidance in this section should help you do this better by:

- providing a general outline of the essay question
- identifying the different types of essay question
- demonstrating how to plan your answer
- demonstrating how to write effective introductions, main paragraphs and conclusions
- explaining the mark scheme.

Answering a Section A question

The essay question: a general outline

For Section A of the examination you are required to select one of two essay questions to answer. For Option D1 (From Kaiser to Führer: Germany 1900–45), the essay questions will be drawn from the following areas:

- The Second Reich – society and government in Germany, c1900–19: economic expansion; political and social tensions; the impact of the First World War.
- The democratic experiment, 1919–29: crises and survival, 1919–24; Stresemann and recovery; the 'Golden Years' of the Weimar Republic; Weimar culture.
- The rise of the Nazis: origins to 1928; impact of the slump in town and country, 1928–33; growing support; coming to power.
- Life in wartime Germany, 1939–45: opposition and conformity; persecution of the Jews and the development of the idea of the 'Final Solution'; the efficiency of the war economy.

From the outset, it is very important to realise that an essay question can be set on one or more of these topics. For example, the essay question on the left, top, focuses on knowledge that is based almost entirely on the second bullet point in the text above, although you might make use of some knowledge of bullet point three in your assessment.

However, the question on the left, bottom, requires knowledge that is based on the second and third bullet points in the text above.

The essay question is marked against Assessment Objective 1a and 1b (AO1a and b), which means that you need to select relevant historical knowledge from what you have learned and use it to support an argument leading to a judgement on the question that has been set. In the exam, you should spend approximately 50 minutes (including about 5 minutes planning) answering the essay question. It is worth 30 marks.

Example essay questions

How far do you agree with the view that the period of 1924 to 1929 was one of both political stability and genuine recovery?

To what extent was the rise of the Nazi Party a result of the economic problems Weimar Germany had faced since 1919?

Recognising the different types of essay question

Section A essay questions are divided into:

- causal questions – requiring you to write an analysis of the causes or causes and consequences of an historical event or development

- judgement questions – requiring you to make and justify an historical judgement about the significance of a particular event, individual or development.

Causal questions

There are three main types of causal question that can appear in Section A.

1. Single-focus

A single-focus causal question requires an explanation for one event, issue or episode. The causal analysis is demanded in the question on the right, top, because of the need to analyse and explain 'Why …?'

2. Double-focus

The double-focus causal question requires you to consider two specific sets of causes or reasons. In the example on the right, centre, you must focus on 'weaknesses in the Weimar political system' and 'economic problems'. You must cover both parts of the question adequately or your answer will be unbalanced.

3. Indirect

An indirect causal question does not have an obvious causal question stem. It makes a claim about causes, which you assess by examining the causes stated in the question and other causes drawn from your own knowledge. In the question on the right, bottom, for instance, any consideration of 'broader political and economic problems' should lead on to a discussion of issues such as economic problems from 1928 onwards and their consequences, and the actions of other Weimar politicians.

Causal questions: dos and don'ts

Do	Don't
✓ Establish clearly the relative importance of the causal factors considered – *this is very important.*	✗ Attempt to use a narrative structure to answer a causal question.
✓ Show, where relevant, how causal factors interacted.	
✓ Structure your essay around the causal factors selected for discussion.	

1. Single-focus

Why was Hitler able to become Chancellor of Germany in 1933?

2. Double-focus

'Weaknesses in the Weimar political system were more important than economic problems in explaining why Hitler became Chancellor in 1933.'
How far do you agree with this view?

3. Indirect

'Hitler's becoming Chancellor in 1933 owed more to broader economic and political problems in Germany than to the actions of the Nazi Party.'
How far do you agree with this view?

1. One-part

> *'In the years 1919–33, the Weimar Constitution was a success.'*
> *How far do you agree with this view?*

2. Two-part

> *How far do you agree with the view that the period of 1924 to 1929 was one of both political stability and genuine recovery?*

3. Causes/consequences

> *To what extent were the weaknesses of the Weimar Republic determined by its constitution?*

4. Change

> *To what extent did political and economic conditions in Germany improve over the period 1919–29?*

5. Mixed

> *Why, and how profoundly, did opposition to the Nazi regime increase during the period 1939–45?*

Judgement questions

Judgement questions typically start: 'To what extent …?', 'How far do you agree that …?', 'How important …?' or 'Examine the validity of the claim that …'.

There are five main types of judgement question that may appear in Section A.

1. One-part

You are required to put forward and support a *single* judgement. In this case (top, left), you need to make a judgement about the extent to which the Weimar Constitution was a success in the given period.

2. Two-part

You are required to offer and support *two separate* judgements. In the example on the left, you need to consider and reach a judgement on the 'political stability' and 'genuine recovery' aspects of the period 1924 to 1929. A constructive approach to this type of question is to split the main analysis into two separate sections, to offer and support a judgement on each aspect.

3. Causes/consequences

Some judgement questions, as in the example on the left, may ask you to make a judgement about causes and/or consequences.

4. Change

Other judgement questions may ask you to make a judgement about the extent or nature of change over a given period. In the example on the left, you are asked to make a judgement about the extent to which conditions improved in the ten years following the establishment of the Weimar Republic. With this type of question it is important to establish clear criteria that you will use to measure the extent or nature of change.

5. Mixed

Occasionally, mixed causal and judgement questions can appear in Section A, as per the example on the left, bottom. With this type of question, you could divide your answer into two sections. One part should analyse the causes and the other should offer and support a judgement.

Judgement questions: dos and don'ts

Do	Don't
✓ Make an explicit judgement that clearly answers the question set (e.g. The Weimar Constitution was/was a partial/wasn't a success in the years 1919–29) – *this is very important.*	✗ Attempt to use a narrative structure to answer a judgement question.
✓ Structure your essay around the analytical points selected for discussion.	✗ Forget to offer an overall judgement.
✓ Show, where relevant, the links between the analytical points that have been developed in the process of forming a judgement.	✗ Offer an implicit or brief judgement.

Planning your answer

Causal questions

When planning an answer to a causal question, it is very important that you follow these steps:

- Structure your answer on the causal factors selected.

- Show how causal factors interacted.

- Establish the relative importance of the causal factors considered.

The diagram below shows some of the relevant causal factors that you could select to answer the causal question on the right.

Example causal question

Why was Hitler able to become Chancellor of Germany in 1933?

Although the **economic and political crisis** that developed was in part a result of the economic and social problems that grew after the collapse of 1929 and intensified with the financial crisis of 1931, it can be argued that the collapse of the 'grand coalition' in March 1930 and the subsequent failings of Brüning's government led to political inertia, with Nazi support growing as successive leaders appeared unable to deal with the developing economic and social crisis.

The **political intrigue** that took place during 1932 was also crucial in bringing Hitler to the Chancellorship. Whilst Nazi electoral popularity had declined to an extent in November 1932, the deals that were cut between Hindenburg, von Papen, von Schleicher and others ultimately saw Hitler benefit from the misguided actions of members of the conservative elite that failed to see beyond their political rivalries.

Why was Hitler able to become Chancellor of Germany in 1933?

The ability of Hitler and the Nazi Party to present themselves as the only group able to deal with the problems Germany faced was also important, with the party organisation proving adaptable to maximise support, whilst their willingness to shape their ideological beliefs to appeal to a range of Germans from the *Mittlestand*, rural voters and other sections of society. Thus electoral support grew partly in protest at the failure of Weimar politics but also as a result of **Nazi success in portraying themselves as the only party that appealed to the nation** rather than sectional or class interests.

Constitutional issues were important in bringing Hitler to power. Although coalitions had endured difficulties during the 1920s, the system had failed to mature to a point where parties could put aside interests in order to agree on a course of action to deal with the problems faced from the early 1930s. Perhaps more significantly, the shift to presidential government, the dissolutions of the Reichstag and the use of Article 48 played into Nazi hands by tarnishing attitudes to democracy, increasing fears over the social order and legitimising a more authoritarian form of government.

An effective plan here would be as follows:

- Structure the main section into four paragraphs, each of which would analyse the role played by one of the selected causal factors in bringing about Hitler's accession to the office of Chancellor.

- Show where the factors interact, for example, the failure of Weimar politicans to deal effectively with the problems of the Great Depression was partly a result of constitutional issues that, in turn, became more significant during the crisis years.

- Establish the relative importance of the causal factors considered; for example, you could argue that the ability of Hitler and the Nazi Party to portray themselves as the only group able to deal with the problems Germany faced was more important than constitutional issues, as these played to the concerns of much of the electorate and to key members of the political elite, whereas the constitutional weaknesses had existed previously without bringing about the effective collapse of democracy.

Example judgement question

'In the years 1919–33, the Weimar Constitution was a success.'
How far do you agree with this view?

Judgement questions

When planning an answer to a judgement question, it is very important that you follow these steps:

- Make an explicit judgement that clearly answers the question set.
- Structure your essay around the analytical points selected for discussion.
- Show, where relevant, the links between the analytical points that have been developed in the process of forming a judgement.

The spectrum below shows a partially completed 'judgement continuum' that would help you to answer the judgement question on the left.

Failure	Partial success/failure	Success
Article 48 set a dangerous precedent from Brüning onwards	PR – coalitions not inherently weak; did often produce weak government	Genuinely democratic, parties represented a range of interests

This judgement continuum is an excellent planning tool because it:

- focuses on the critical element – making a judgement
- allows you to put the historical evidence into relevant judgement categories that provide an ideal structure for the main section of your essay.

Once completed, the spectrum will help you to reach an overall judgement.

With this particular question, after you have placed all the relevant evidence from the period in the appropriate judgement category (success/failure), you are then in a position to make an overall judgement on the extent of success. This could be based, for example, on the category containing the largest amount of evidence. Alternatively, it might be based on the date of the evidence in each category (for example, early 1920s evidence indicates 'success' but later in the 1920s and early 1930s evidence reveals more of a 'failure').

Writing effective introductions, main paragraphs and conclusions

The introduction

A good introduction is very important when you are answering an essay question, partly because it is the first impression you make with the examiner. Treat it as a golden opportunity to impress with your understanding of what the question is asking you to do and how you aim to answer it. Spend about 5–7 minutes – but no longer – writing this opening paragraph. A good introduction should aim to fulfil these functions:

- set out clearly your understanding of what the question is asking you to do
- identify the range of factors you intend to discuss in the main section
- offer a provisional judgement, so the examiner knows the line of argument you intend to take
- define any key words in the question and explain the significance of any dates that have been included.

The passage below is a strong introduction to the question on the right:

> While the Nazi regime appeared dominant in the early years of the war, as they had beforehand, with no effective opposition, threats did exist and in many ways grew as the early successes of the war stalled and were ultimately reversed. The army did offer the greatest potential for a realistic threat, in terms of organisation, force and proximity to the regime, and thus growing dissatisfaction within the army was significant, particularly when considered against the fragmented nature of other opposition groups, such as those on the left or dissenting youth groups, or the largely mild opposition which stemmed from the churches and conservative elites. However, although opponents in the army did grow to be a real threat and indeed came close to toppling Hitler, the inertia of the wider military in its reluctance to turn against the regime meant they were easily emasculated. Thus it must be said that whilst they offered the most credible threat in terms of the likely success of an assassination attempt, in the wider sense the threat was limited.

Example question

'During the period 1939–45, opponents within the army posed a greater threat to Hitler and the Nazi regime than any other opposition group.'
How far do you agree with this statement?

This is an effective introduction for three reasons:

1. It sets out briefly but clearly what constitutes a 'threat', in terms of the question – it shows what it would take to effectively challenge and threaten the Nazi regime. This immediately indicates that the student has a clear grasp of the issue to be explained, giving an indication of the criteria that will be used for assessment.

2. The middle section clearly identifies the threat from opponents within the army and two other relevant opposition groups that will be analysed to reach a judgement on the 'greater threat'.

3. The final sentences offer a provisional judgement about the extent to which the army was the 'greater threat'.

The main section
The main section is a crucial part of your essay because this is where you develop the detailed analysis essential for answering the question. Try to write four to six substantial paragraphs in this part of your response. Each paragraph in the main section should:

- support the opening point with examples from your own knowledge and then make clear how this adds weight to your argument (**Point–Evidence–Explanation–Evaluation**)
- address a new point

- link back to previous points, where possible, to show that you understand the connections

- follow on naturally from the one before.

Finish each point by linking back to the wording of the question in some way. This should guarantee that you are addressing the question directly.

Following the 'opposition' question on page 101, this is a good main section paragraph.

> Where the threat of the army can be seen to have grown is from 1943 onwards, as failures in wartime meant many more within the officer ranks questioned Hitler's stewardship. In the period 1943–44, there were at least six planned attempts on Hitler's life by serving military officers, including the failed timed device planted on Hitler's flight to Rastenburg. While these all ultimately failed, it offered the most realistic chance of toppling Hitler, as the army had the autonomy, means and opportunity to pose a realistic assassination threat. In turn, this was the greatest chance of a wider coup as, for many reluctant opponents, their objection to a coup was its disloyalty to the state and office; with Hitler gone, the officer class would have been likely to step in. That the perpetrators were generally treated better, being shielded by their own circle in the aborted attempts before the Nazis discovered the plots highlights the potential strength of the army. Army officers could foment opposition, as even if suspected, they were unlikely to face the arbitrary justice of a People's Court without hard evidence. However, as wartime failure increased the suspicion of the Gestapo towards army plots, Hitler's protection was increased accordingly. The Stauffenberg bomb plot was in this sense a last realistic attempt; it was only by fortune that Hitler survived, and so in terms of Hitler personally it was the greatest threat. The resulting crackdown emasculated the army, with hundreds executed and Himmler appointed Commander-in-Chief. However, even this highlights the potential the army had to threaten, if the will had been there. Only 22 of over 2000 generals were removed. While this highlights the isolated nature of resistance within the army, it is likely many more of doubtful loyalty escaped harm, and stands in stark contrast to the kind of widespread purge that would have threatened any other opposition group.

This is an effective main section paragraph for the following reasons:

- It begins by introducing the central point – the growing threat the army did pose from 1943.

- It offers clear explanations of why this was and was not a threat, examining argument and counter-argument to the point raised.

- It includes relevant evidence to support explanations.

- Finally, it provides an evaluation as to the extent to which the army did pose a threat to the Nazi regime in this period.

The conclusion

For A2 level, the conclusion has to be more than a summary of what you have said. Rather, it needs to be the culmination of your understanding of issues established in the introduction, the arguments examined and assessed, and the evaluative judgement resulting from this. Don't skimp on this section; spend a good 5 minutes on it. For many students it may be the key part of the essay in determining the level awarded, as it is where you actually answer the question and weigh up your analysis.

A good conclusion will:

- round off all the points you have already made in your argument and make it clear why you have argued your case in this particular way

- reach a clear judgement, for example, the relative importance of factors

- consider the themes running through your essay and how they link, demonstrating your understanding that historical issues and factors do not act in isolation to each other

- avoid throwing in a brand new point at this stage – it's too late!

Still on the 'opposition' question, this is a strong conclusion.

In conclusion, the army can be seen to have been the greatest threat to the regime, insofar as it was opposition from within this group that came the closest to actually killing Hitler. However, such a judgement is marginal; assassination attempts aside, all of these groups struggled to offer effective opposition, as the opportunity for organised resistance was limited by the authorities. The left and youth opposition was arguably the most motivated, but their limited resources and fractured groups could only offer sporadic resistance, while the churches had widespread support and were hard for even the Nazis to close down, but as institutions they did not really attempt to threaten the regime. The officer ranks of the army had an advantage in that they were indispensable to the regime, but when some of their number did break their conservative mindsets to attempt to overthrow Hitler, their resistance was easily quashed, so while they were the greater threat, this was still limited.

This is an effective conclusion because of the following points:

- It begins its overall judgement by assessing the extent to which the army was the 'greater threat' to Hitler and the Nazi regime in the years 1939–45.

- It then moves on to examine the balance of this judgement, weighing the relative threat posed by the army against other opposition groups. A sophisticated feature here is the consideration of the nature of the different threats, examining issues such as the strength and size of groups, proximity to Hitler and the motivation they had as opponents – returning to criteria for how the 'greater threat' is judged.

- The final sentence clearly reiterates the key judgement.

Understanding the mark scheme

The examiner puts each essay into one of five levels, according to the criteria in the table overleaf. Your answer is then moved within the level (low, mid or high), depending on how well it meets the descriptor.

Obviously, you want your answer to go into the highest possible level, therefore it is worth becoming familiar with the table, so that you know what the examiners are looking for.

Level	Level descriptor	Descriptor comments	Comments/example
Level 1 Simple statements 1–6 marks	Students will produce a series of statements, some of which may be simplified. The statements will be supported by factual material, which has some accuracy and relevance although not directed at the focus of the question. The material will be mostly generalised. Low: 1–2 marks, mid: 3–4 marks, high: 5–6 marks	A level 1 answer is typically based on a limited amount of material and deals with the topic rather than the focus of the question. Knowledge is generalised with few examples to support the statements.	A typical level 1 response to the question: *'How far do you agree with the view that the period of 1924 to 1929 was one of both political stability and genuine recovery?'* would contain material about the period 1924 to 1929 but would not address the focus of 'political stability' or 'genuine recovery'.
Level 2 Statements with some development 7–12 marks	Students will produce statements with some development in the form of mostly accurate and relevant factual material. There will be some analysis, but focus on the analytical demand of the question will be largely implicit. Candidates will attempt to make links between the statements and the material but is unlikely to be developed very far. Low: 7–8 marks, mid: 9–10 marks, high: 11–12 marks	Level 2 answers can provide reasonably extensive information but often in the form of a narrative or a description. There is some attempt to link the material to the question but it will not be explicit, links are assumed and/or the answer is narrative. The range of evidence is limited and links are asserted, rather than supported with information.	A level 2 response to the question given above, for example, will contain statements on the period 1924 to 1929 that will have either only implicit reference to stability or recovery, or arguments based on insufficient evidence. Links to the question focus will be asserted, rather than shown. The student may maintain that under Stresemann there was a recovery, but without offering developed comments; for example, assuming it to be self-evident that the Stresemann years were 'golden'.
Level 3 Attempts analysis 13–18 marks	Students' answers will be broadly analytical and will show some understanding of the focus of the question. They may, however, include material, which is either descriptive, and thus only implicitly relevant to the question's focus, or which strays from that focus in places. Factual material will be accurate, but it may not consistently display depth and/or relevance. Low: 13–14 marks, mid: 15–16 marks, high: 17–18 marks	In a level 3 response, the majority of the paragraphs will have a relevant point, some supporting evidence and related comments linked to the question. There will, however, be some weaker passages that may drift into narrative, lack a clear link to the question, include irrelevant material or lack analytical depth.	A typical level 3 response to the question stated above will contain paragraphs with relevant analysis (on, perhaps, the impact coalition politics had on the political stability in this period). It will also have weaker passages (such as a narrative section on, say, foreign loans and the economy). It may also be significantly imbalanced, for example, mostly on stability, very little on recovery.

Level	Level descriptor	Descriptor comments	Comments/example
Level 4 Analytical response 19–24 marks	Students offer an analytical response, which relates well to the focus of the question and which shows some understanding of the key issues contained in it with some evaluation of argument. The analysis will be supported by accurate factual material, which will be mostly relevant to the question asked. The selection of material may lack balance in places. Low: 19–20 marks, mid: 21–22 marks, high: 23–24 marks	At level 4, a student's response will offer an analysis of the issues raised by the question. The answer draws out the key points with detailed knowledge used to develop an argument. There may be a little drifting from the specific question or a lack of balance, with some aspects dealt with only briefly; the response may be a bit inconsistent. The answer will show some attempt to evaluate the evidence used in the argument.	A level 4 answer to the question given on page 104 will deal with both issues (political stability and genuine recovery) and explore arguments and issues for and against both of them. The student will also appreciate that there is both overlap and distinction between these two terms. The answer will not lose sight of the question focus but it may lack balance.
Level 5 Sustained analysis 25–30 marks	Students offer a sustained analysis, which directly addresses the focus of the question. They demonstrate explicit understanding of the key issues raised by the question, evaluating arguments and – as appropriate – interpretations. The analysis will be supported by an appropriate range and depth of accurate and well-selected factual material. Low: 25–26 marks, mid: 27–28 marks, high: 29–30 marks	At level 5, the student's analysis is developed, balanced and sustained. The answer draws out the key points and develops an argument with detailed knowledge. The answer is well structured and discusses the evidence used to support, reject or modify the statement in the question. The answer evaluates the interpretations and arguments.	In the question on page 104, a level 5 answer will fully explore a range of issues. For example, in examining the view that, through the given period, coalitions were returned that demonstrated moderate parties working effectively, but were not maturing in such a way that could meet more serious challenges, there was a stability, but of a rather temporary nature, and that these can be linked to other political issues, such as the role of the President, as well as the relationship between these issues and the economic recovery. Thus, the implications of political stability will be explored beyond the issues of proportional representation and coalitions to weigh critically the various issues relating to political stability. The response will offer an evaluative analysis with a balanced debate on the proposition contained in the question.

Answering a Section B question

The Section B question has a different focus than the Section A question. In the Section A question you are required to use your own knowledge (AO1) to complete the answer. In contrast, the Section B question requires you to reach a judgement about a claim by integrating your own knowledge (AO1) with interpretations offered by the sources (AO2b).

The Section B question focuses on the two controversies studied:

a) To what extent was Germany responsible for the outbreak of the First World War?

b) How popular and efficient was the Nazi regime in the years 1933–9?

You must select from two questions, each of which refers to one of these controversies. Each question will be accompanied by three secondary sources. The sources will offer different interpretations relating to the controversies that you have studied.

Choosing the question

Begin by reading both questions. If you immediately have a clear preference, skim-read the three sources that accompany that question (looking for key words, names and dates, and ensuring that you understand the interpretations offered) before you commit yourself.

Significantly, questions often contain a quote from one of the sources or paraphrase an interpretation put forward by a source. Therefore, it is a good idea to start by identifying the source referred to in the question. Skim-reading and looking for the source referred to in the question should enable you to check that you have understood the question correctly, and will help you as you plan your answer.

If you have no clear preference, then read the sources for each question carefully and base your choice on which set of sources you can understand most clearly. You should have left yourself 1 hour and 10 minutes to complete this question, so you can spend 5 minutes making sure that you have made the right choice.

Planning your answer

Once you have selected the question it is very important to spend some time planning your answer. To access level 3 or above, you need to link your own knowledge to the sources. It is almost impossible to do this successfully without planning. Make sure that you leave enough time to do this and remember to think carefully about the main issues raised by the question. You can find an example of a plan on page 111.

How do you work out the interpretation of the sources?

All of the sources in this Unit will be secondary sources. Your task is to understand the interpretations they offer. Therefore, it is useful to highlight and annotate the sources as you read them.

Some sources will contain more than one interpretation. For example, they may contain an argument and a counter-argument. Other sources may only offer one interpretation. In either case, it is crucial to understand the interpretation the source offers.

It is important to work out which sources support and challenge the interpretation offered in the question. You could use different colours to indicate this:

- Use one colour to indicate the parts of the source that *support the interpretation* offered in the question (yellow highlighting is used in the examples on pages 107–08).
- Use a second colour to indicate the parts of the source that *contradict the interpretation* offered in the question (green highlighting is used in the examples on pages 107–08).
- Use a third colour to indicate the parts of the source that offer an *alternative interpretation* (blue highlighting is used in the example on page 108).

Example question

How far do you agree with the view that Germany's aggressive actions were chiefly responsible for the outbreak of the First World War?

Source 1
(From David Blackbourn, *History of Germany 1780–1918*, published by Blackwell Publishing 2002)

German responsibility for war should not be restricted to the issue of whether Bethmann, or the German government, or the Kaiser, desired peace in 1912–14 or, for that matter, earlier. Of course they would have preferred to get what they wanted without war. But German actions going back to the 1890s had done much to create international tension. Bethmann personally was a sensitive, passive, fatalistic man, but he was faced with reaping the whirlwind sown by his predecessors. Others bore more responsibility, like Tirpitz, who built a battle fleet aimed at the British but professed his peaceful intentions.

Agreement with the interpretation offered by the question:

- 'German responsibility for war should not be restricted to the issue of whether Bethmann, or the German government, or the Kaiser, desired peace in 1912–14'
- 'German actions going back to the 1890s had done much to create international tension'
- 'Others bore more responsibility, like Tirpitz, who built a battle fleet aimed at the British.'

Contradiction to the interpretation offered by the question:

- 'Of course they would have preferred to get what they wanted without war.'

This method helps you identify arguments, issues and information that relate to the interpretation in the question.

Some of the points identified above are straightforward in their support of the arguments, for example, Blackbourn's argument that 'German actions going back to the 1890s had done much to create international tension' clearly indicates German responsibility towards the outbreak of war, albeit not necessarily 'chiefly'.

Others, such as the first bullet point, invite a more developed exploration of the topic. Blackbourn's point regarding the 'issue of whether' German leaders 'desired peace in 1912–14' suggests there is debate over the matter. The extent to which they desired peace can be discussed. If this is accepted to some degree, the extent to which they still risked war even if they desired peace can be explored.

Although parts of the source can be selected in this way, they should also be read carefully in the context of the full extract, to make sense of their meaning.

Now repeat the exercise, using the following source:

> **Source 2**
> (From L.F.C. Turner, *The Origins of the First World War*, published by W.W. Norton 1970)
>
> After Sarajevo, Wilhelm II and Bethmann-Hollweg courted a great war and, in view of the prevailing mood in Paris and St Petersburg, there was little hope of averting catastrophe after the Austrian ultimatum was presented in Belgrade. The crisis got out of control because Bethmann pushed Austria into a premature declaration of war on Serbia. The French General Staff drove Russia along the fatal path to mobilization. This conduct reflected French confidence in victory, but was also a reaction to the German war plan devised by Count von Schlieffen. That plan, with its flagrant violations of neutrality, had been approved by the German Government since 1904. In the final phase, military considerations were of decisive importance.

Agreement with the interpretation offered by the question (yellow):

- 'After Sarajevo, Wilhelm II and Bethmann-Hollweg courted a great war'
- 'The crisis got out of control because Bethmann pushed Austria into a premature declaration of war on Serbia'
- 'This conduct … was also a reaction to the German war plan devised by Count von Schlieffen … with its flagrant violations of neutrality … approved by the German Government since 1904.'

Alternative interpretation offered by the source (blue):

- 'in view of the prevailing mood in Paris and St Petersburg, there was little hope of averting catastrophe'
- 'The French General Staff drove Russia along the fatal path to mobilization'
- 'French confidence in victory.'

Again, evidence can be found to suggest German responsibility for the outbreak of the First World War, although here the focus is more on the actions of German leaders during the July Crisis, shaped by longer-term concerns manifested in the Schlieffen Plan.

However, Turner additionally points towards an alternative interpretation, highlighting French responsibility through their encouragement of Russian mobilisation, even in the knowledge that this would be likely to result in war.

The alternative interpretation can be highlighted in a third colour as, while it can be used to counter the original interpretation offered by the question, it does so more by offering a different explanation as to what lay behind war, rather than directly refuting the original claim.

While such distinctions may not always be fully clear, attempting to plan in this way will give your essay breadth and ensure it is organised around debating the differing interpretations offered by the sources. Other parts of the source could also be identified and used to develop such an answer.

Integrating sources and cross-referencing

It is really important that you do not simply work through the sources one by one, because this kind of answer is unlikely to achieve more than level 2 in either Assessment Objective. You should try to treat the sources as a set and use them together. You will find that there are points of disagreement between the interpretations offered by the sources, as well as points of agreement. Where possible, you should cross-reference these points.

To help you to understand how to go about the task of integration, you will be examining Source 3, together with those above.

> **Source 3**
>
> (From Niall Ferguson, *The Pity of War*, published by Allen Lane 1998)
>
> The extent of German malice aforethought must not be exaggerated. For men who have been accused of planning a war, the senior members of the German General Staff were uncannily relaxed in July 1914. At the time the Kaiser issued his famous 'blank cheque' to the Austrians, Moltke, Waldersee, Groener, chief of the Railway Section, and Major Nicolai, the head of key intelligence agency Section 111b, were all on holiday (in separate resorts, it should be said). Tirpitz and Admiral von Pohl were too. It was only on 16th July that Nicolai's stand-in, Captain Kurt Neuhof, was advised to step up surveillance of Russian military activity. Nicolai himself was not back at his desk for another two days. Even then his orders to the so-called 'tension travellers' – i.e. German spies in Russia and France – were merely to find out 'whether war preparations are taking place in France and Russia'.

Begin by looking for areas of agreement and disagreement between the sources.

Ways in which the sources agree:

- Sources 1 and 2 both focus on German responsibility. Source 1 emphasises more issues dating back to the 19th century, while Source 2 focuses on the summer of 1914. Both sources do highlight the debate over Bethmann's actions.

- Sources 1 and 2 also both give examples of policies and decisions made further back, by Tirpitz and Schlieffen, that suggest responsibility and indeed may be used to argue Bethmann's room for manoeuvre was limited.

- Sources 2 and 3 both highlight Germany's 'blank cheque' to the Austrians, focusing on the events of the July Crisis and suggesting some level of Austrian involvement, although they are far from agreement over who should shoulder the responsibility within this period and pairing.

Ways in which the sources disagree:

- Sources 2 and 3 place different levels of importance on the role of Germany during the July Crisis, with Source 3 seeing German leaders as demonstrating little evidence of a desire for war, while Source 2 stresses Bethmann and Germany as being the prime actors in these events.

- Sources 1 and 2 are different in that Source 1 stresses the significance of the responsibility created by Germany's actions, while Source 2 emphasises poor decision-making during the crisis of 1914.

- Source 3 is clearly at odds with Sources 1 and 2, to some extent, in arguing that Germany showed little preparation for war during this period.

The role of your own knowledge

Although the sources will drive your argument, you need to include relevant, specific and detailed own knowledge to support your argument. You can use own knowledge in three main ways:

1. You can expand on a point that has already been made in the sources. For example, you could pick up on Source 1's point that Tirpitz 'built a battle fleet aimed at the British but professed his peaceful intentions' by examining the policy of *Flottenpolitik*, and the extent to which this was responsible for increasing tension through provoking the Anglo–German naval race and influencing the development of the *Entente* and subsequent developments.

2. You can challenge a point that has been made in the sources. For example, Source 3 argues that the 'relaxed' nature of German military leaders suggests little desire for war at this point. However, you could use your own knowledge to point out that the stage of the crisis Ferguson refers to was before many of the key developments in the crisis, with the Tsar still seeking restraint on behalf of Germany in its support of Austria, and German plans anyway being firmly established through the Schlieffen Plan. This could also be considered in the light of interpretations to suggest that, while Ferguson is correct to point to the relaxed behaviour of military planners, Bethmann's actions were a calculated risk to fight a limited war if attempts to gain advantage through diplomatic measures were unsuccessful.

3. Finally, you can use your own knowledge of the controversy to put forward an interpretation that is not mentioned in the sources, but draws on information provided by the sources. For example, Source 1 mentions the issue of whether the 'Kaiser desired peace in 1912–14', without developing this interpretation. You could use your own knowledge of the controversy to explore Fritz Fischer's arguments that the decisions placing Germany on the path to war had already been decided by 1912.

The following excerpt is an example of how to integrate sources and own knowledge. Source material appears in black, own knowledge appears in blue. Note how well the student uses knowledge to develop and explore the point that, even if they were not outright aggressors, the actions of German leaders carried the risk of war.

> In this sense, while Turner argues Bethmann 'courted a great war', he was more the 'passive' character that Blackbourn portrays as 'reaping the whirlwind of his predecessors'. The likes of Bülow, who planned a 'successful foreign policy to rally and unite' Germans, had done more to stir pan-German sentiment and create a policy which, whilst not strictly aggressive, was clumsy brinkmanship

which did 'create' the 'international tension' Blackbourn considers, with Tirpitz's actions being the greatest example of this. His naval strategy, aimed at forcing Britain to concentrate on home ports and so allow Germany greater opportunity to exploit colonial ambition, backfired insofar as it brought Britain's focus on Europe in a different way, leading to the *Entente* that German statesmen thought near impossible. Blackbourn is correct that while they 'preferred to get what they wanted without war', the War Council of 1912 shows that at the very least they were prepared to risk war in committing to support Austro–Hungary.

When you are using your own knowledge to develop a point in the sources, make sure you link the point clearly to your discussion of the sources. The easiest way to do this is to add your own knowledge to your plan once you have finished studying the sources. You could plan in two colours, using one for the sources and another for own knowledge.

Producing a plan

Your plan should focus on the interpretations put forward in the sources. It should also integrate sources and own knowledge. A plan for the question discussed on pages 106–11 could look like the example shown below. Own knowledge is shown in blue panels, interpretations from the sources in orange panels and evidence from the sources in green panels.

Own knowledge
Bülow's *Weltpolitik* and pan-Germanism led to 'risk policy'; result was clumsy brinkmanship that backfired causing tensions and increasing British involvement in Europe

Sources 1 & 2
Bethmann limited by 'the whirlwind sown by his predecessors'; tension increased by the likes of Tirpitz (Source 1). German military 'considerations … decisive', thus Schlieffen, Kaiser and advisers should bear a degree of blame (Source 2)

Paragraph 1
Source 1
German actions and policy from 1890 were responsible

Source 2
Bethmann's courting of war through pushing Austria in declaring war on Serbia

Paragraph 2
Sources 2 & 3
Germany's actions during the July Crisis were responsible

Source 3
That the 'senior members of the German General Staff were uncannily relaxed' challenges the view of German responsibility

Own knowledge
Kaiser Wilhelm's insistence on supporting Austria–Hungary at the Potsdam meeting on 5 July, arguments that Bethmann had limited control over the actions of the General Staff

How far do you agree with the view that Germany's aggressive actions were chiefly responsible for the outbreak of the First World War?

Sources 1 & 2
Source 2 emphasises consequences of alliances in shaping actions of members after Sarajevo. Source 1 could be used to explore link between the naval race and the development of alliances (also link to Source 3)

Paragraph 4
Sources 1, 2 & 3
The alliance system and increasing militarism were responsible

Paragraph 3
Sources 2 & 3
German actions were defensive in response to fears of encirclement

Source 2
French confidence and urging of Russia encouraged Russian mobilisation (link to Source 3)

Own knowledge
The loss of connection with Russia, the development of the Franco–Russian alliance from 1894 or the *Entente* from 1904 could all be explored, as could Germany's own increasing dependence on its ties with Austria

Own knowledge
Examine Zechlin & Erdmann's arguments, e.g. the use of Riezler's diary evidence to suggest no systematic war planning existed from 1912

Look back at the information on pages 100–03 to remind yourself of the importance of constructing effective introductions, main paragraphs and conclusions.

Reaching a developed judgement

Bear in mind that your essay is weighing up an interpretation. Therefore, you will need to reach a judgement regarding that claim as part of your essay. Think carefully about whether you agree or disagree with the claim made in the question. Ideally, you will reach a view before you begin writing the essay and argue your case throughout the essay. Remember, though, that you must take account of the points that *challenge* as well as those that support your case. Remember, too, that you are not *evaluating* the sources, you are using your own knowledge and evidence from other sources to examine the claims that they are making.

The examiner is not looking for a particular answer. Rather, the examiner will be looking at the quality of your argument and the way you use the sources and your own knowledge during your argument.

Key tips for structuring your answer

Do	Don't
✓ Read both questions and check that you understand their focus before selecting which to answer.	✗ Begin to write without planning.
✓ Plan your answer carefully – use different coloured pens to indicate sources and own knowledge.	✗ Describe what the sources say.
	✗ Work through the sources in sequence, without cross-referencing them with one another.
✓ Reach a judgement about how far you agree with the statement in the question before beginning your essay. Develop a clear argument that supports your judgement throughout the essay.	✗ Provide your own knowledge in a separate section of the essay to your discussion of the sources.
✓ Focus directly on the question throughout your essay.	✗ Discuss the provenance and reliability of the sources.
✓ Examine the sources looking for evidence that:	✗ Forget to link the points you make to the question you are answering.
✓ supports the claim made in the question	✗ Write an essay mainly from your own knowledge, ignoring the sources.
✓ contradicts the claim made in the question	✗ Describe the way historians' views differ, for example, over the causes of the First World War, rather than answering the question that has been set.
✓ offers an alternative interpretation to the one offered in the question.	✗ Fail to reach a judgement in your conclusion.
✓ Cross-reference the sources.	
✓ Integrate the sources with your own knowledge throughout the essay. Use your own knowledge to develop interpretations offered by the sources, to counter interpretations offered by the sources and to offer new interpretations.	
✓ Make sure your essay reaches a judgement regarding the interpretation offered by the question. Do this by weighing up the interpretations offered by the sources and your own knowledge.	

Understanding the mark scheme

The mark scheme means that you are required to show a number of skills. You need to be aware of the requirements of the question and how the mark scheme works in order to maximise your chances of doing well.

The Assessment Objectives

Section B counts for 40 of the 70 marks. It examines two Assessment Objectives:

- First, your essay is marked against Assessment Objective 1a and 1b (AO1a and b), for a possible 16 marks. It assesses your ability to select relevant historical knowledge from what you have learned and your ability to use it to support an argument leading to a judgement about the question that has been set. This is the same skill as in Section A (see pages 104–05). However, Section B includes sources, so you will have to integrate source material with your own knowledge.

- Second, your essay is marked against Assessment Objective 2b (AO2b), for a possible 24 marks. It assesses your ability to analyse and evaluate judgements about the past. In this context, this means analysing and evaluating the interpretations provided by the sources. It does not require you to consider the reliability of the sources.

The mark scheme for AO2b

Level	Level descriptor	Descriptor comments	Comments/example
Level 1 1–4 marks	The students will comprehend the surface features of sources and select from them in order to identify points, which support or differ from the view posed in the question. When reaching a decision in relation to the question, the sources will be used singly and in the form of a summary of their information. Own knowledge of the issue under debate will be presented as information but not integrated with the provided material. Low: 1–2 marks, high: 3–4 marks	A level 1 answer will generally contain a few brief quotations lifted from the sources, which have not always been understood. It is very likely that the student will have worked through the sources in sequence.	A typical level 1 response to the question: 'How far do you agree with the view that Germany's aggressive actions were chiefly responsible for the outbreak of the First World War?' would copy passages from the sources, or paraphrase material from the sources. The sources would not be cross-referenced, or linked to own knowledge and there would be little attempt to answer the question.
Level 2 5–9 marks	Students will comprehend the sources and note points of challenge and support for the stated claim. They will combine the information from the sources to illustrate points linked to the question. Low: 5–6 marks, high: 7–9 marks	A level 2 answer will generally use the sources more extensively and points will be picked out from them that agree or disagree with the view presented in the question. It is still likely to be summarising what the sources say. It may work through the sources in sequence, or begin to use the sources in combination.	A level 2 response to the question given above will begin to focus on the question and will use material from the sources to form a very basic for and against structure. There might be some attempt to cross-reference.

Level	Level descriptor	Descriptor comments	Comments/example
Level 3 10–14 marks	Students will interpret the sources with confidence, showing the ability to analyse some key points of the arguments offered and to reason from the evidence of the sources. They will develop points of challenge and support for the stated claim from the provided source material and deploy material gained from relevant reading and knowledge of the issues under discussion. The answer shows clear understanding that the issue is one of interpretation. Low: 10–11 marks, high: 12–14 marks	A level 3 answer will show an understanding that the sources present differing interpretations in relation to the view expressed in the question. This is likely to be achieved by examining some of the evidence that agrees with the view in the question and then looking at the evidence that disagrees with it. At level 3 the sources will be used mostly to provide information rather than interpretations. The sources will be cross-referenced.	A typical level 3 response to the same question will use information from the sources thematically. It may contain paragraphs on the German aggression and the actions of Germany's leaders, the international system of alliances, the importance of militarism and war planning or the responsibility of other nations.
Level 4 15–19 marks	Students will interpret the sources with confidence showing the ability to understand the basis of the arguments offered by the authors and to relate these to wider knowledge of the issues under discussion. Discussion of the claim in the question proceeds from an exploration of the issues raised by the process of analysing the sources and the extension of these issues from other relevant reading and own knowledge of the points under debate. Students will present an integrated response with developed reasoning and debating of the evidence in order to create judgements in relation to the stated claim, although not all the issues will be fully developed. The students will reach and sustain a conclusion based on the discriminating use of the evidence. Low: 15–16 marks, high: 17–19 marks	A level 4 answer will focus on the interpretations offered by the sources. These will be linked confidently to the wider debate to which the question refers. The sources will be integrated with one another. The essay will arrive at a judgement based on the interpretations offered by the sources and the evidence from own knowledge.	A level 4 response to the question on page 111, using the sources provided on pages 107–09, may well begin by addressing the argument of Source 1, the argument to which the question refers. It could link this to Source 2's suggestion of responsibility during the July Crisis. Students could then link this to their own knowledge to examine the extent to which these were responsible due to aggression or recklessness. Later paragraphs could combine sources and own knowledge to address the other issues raised in the sources and reach a judgement.

Level	Level descriptor	Descriptor comments	Comments/example
Level 5 20–24 marks	Students will interpret the sources with confidence and discrimination, assimilating the author's arguments and displaying independence of thought in the ability to assess the presented views in the light of own knowledge and reading. Treatment of argument and discussion of evidence will show that the full demands of the question have been appreciated and addressed. Students will present a sustained evaluative argument and reach fully substantiated conclusions demonstrating an understanding of the nature of historical debate. Low: 20–21 marks, high: 22–24 marks	A level 5 answer will focus on the interpretations offered by the sources, assimilating these into an overall argument, focused on the question. Material from the sources will be precisely selected and used with confidence. Level 5 answers will assess the interpretations offered by the sources in the light of their own knowledge. Answers will address the full demands of the question and reach a fully substantiated conclusion, based on a sustained argument.	In some ways a level 5 response would be similar to a level 4 response. Both would focus on the question, evaluate the interpretations of the sources and integrate the sources with own knowledge to reach a judgement. However, at level 5 the essay would have an overall argument that runs throughout the essay. Finally, the conclusion would flow naturally from the argument contained in the essay.

Exemplar essays and commentaries

Section A: essay question

How far do you agree with the view that the period 1924 to 1929 was one of both political stability and genuine recovery? **[30 marks]**

This essay question requires you to make and justify an historical judgement about the extent to which the period of 1924 to 1929 was one of stability and recovery in Weimar Germany. An examiner will be looking for:

1. an analytical (not a descriptive) response which focuses on Weimar recovery
2. relevant supporting evidence drawn from across the 1924–9 timeframe
3. an informed assessment of both 'stability' *and* 'recovery' viewpoints
4. a substantiated judgement that supports or challenges the statement in the question.

Grade C student answer

The period of 1924 to 1929 is often seen as the 'Golden Years' of the Weimar Republic, with peace, prosperity and relative stability. An economic recovery took place after the problems of hyperinflation and, while this was later disrupted by the Great Depression from 1929, up to that point the economy seemed to be booming. Similarly, the political system appeared more stable, with fewer elections being required and less of a threat from extremist attacks like had taken place in between 1918–23. However, the political system was still limited by proportional representation, and the threat of the enemies of democracy had not gone away.

Weimar Germany did see political stability over the period 1924–9. After the defeat of the Beer Hall *Putsch* in 1923, there were no significant attacks on the state. Groups such as the Nazis almost disappeared from political life in Germany during most of this period and the activities of groups such as the SA were dramatically reduced. The number of political murders was also hugely reduced after the peak of 1922, which also must be seen as a success. These relative successes gave the Weimar Republic stability in the sense that it was a period of relative calm in which it had the chance to concentrate on establishing genuine democratic roots after the trauma of 1923. ☞

The introduction shows a broad understanding of the demands of the question, setting out aspects of the period in question to outline issues relating to recovery and to stability. There is some attempt to establish potential arguments, such as appearance of stability. Although there is some description of events, this could be improved with a sharper focus on setting out the range of arguments that could be considered, and beginning to establish the criteria that will be used in order to reach judgement on the issues of stability and recovery.

This focused first main paragraph offers a clear argument. A criterion by which to measure stability – 'no significant attacks on the state' – has been made explicit and is supported, using reasonable own knowledge. The paragraph ends with a valid comment regarding the issue of stability, although this could be more effectively directed at the question. To improve further, the point could be examined in more depth to show exactly how far it demonstrates stability and then a judgement reached on this.

The make-up of the Reichstag during 1924–9 is also evidence of political stability. Although proportional representation was still an issue that allowed small parties a foot in the door, extreme parties on the left and right saw their support reduced, with the Nazi share of the vote down to 2.6% by 1928 and the communist parties dramatically reduced from highs of almost 20% of the vote in 1920. The main beneficiaries of this were the moderate parties, with the SPD share increasing to 29.8% in 1928 and the Grand Coalition under Muller from that year commanding a total of over 60% of the seats in the Reichstag, meaning it was able to govern effectively unlike previous minority coalitions. The coalitions were, in the main, able to govern effectively, largely as they did not face the shocks that earlier and later governments faced.

Stability can also be seen to some extent through the continuance in power of key individuals such as Gustav Stresemann. Stresemann may have been reduced to the Foreign Ministry, as his party was a minor part of coalitions from 1924, but he was crucial in the achievements that meant the majority of the German public supported the Weimar Republic in this period. Similarly, while Hindenburg is often considered to have been anti-democratic, tending to seek the DNVP in coalitions rather than the larger left-wing SPD, there was no swing to the right in government policy, and his loyalty to the constitution actually disappointed many who aspired to a more authoritarian Germany.

Weimar Germany did see a real cultural revival in this period. Art, literature and poetry flourished in this period, with many of the works coming out of the Berlin scene rejecting traditional values. Berlin gained a reputation as a place of toleration and creativity, with the paintings of George Grosz being popular for their criticism of the old elites. German cinema also saw huge growth, with directors, such as Fritz Lang, producing the modernist 'Metropolis', and stars such as Marlene Dietrich. The lack of censorship under the Weimar Republic contrasted greatly with the Second Reich, and cabaret and jazz clubs were hugely popular, particularly in Berlin.

The economy did not really see a recovery as it was reliant upon foreign investment. The US loans did produce real growth and allow Germany to make reparations payments, but Germany was heavily dependent upon these, and so the onset of the Wall Street Crash ended what was in reality a fragile recovery. The German economy also had problems during ☞

In this paragraph, the answer is again well focused, offering useful and very specific detail regarding the electoral success of political parties in the period. There is some degree of analysis, explaining the significance of the increased share of the vote for the moderate parties, attempting to highlight the issue of proportional representation and ending with a judgement. However, the judgement could be more explicitly focused on the question – the issue of 'governing effectively' is certainly valid, although this could be more clearly directed towards the issue of stability.

Again, the student offers a focused argument on political stability, which is convincing insofar as it uses specific detail and clear reasoning, as well as being clearly structured around two separate examples. Analysis is offered to a degree, suggesting that the point is not all positive. However, this is implicit.

It could be improved by more explicitly considering the implications of the issues suggested; that is, Hindenburg being anti-democratic, Stresemann being the key figure yet not being Chancellor. These issues could potentially be developed to a very high level by exploring how far they revealed the limitations of the stability. As it is, the student has included three points about political stability, but these are rather one-directional, largely suggesting everything was stable.

This paragraph is weaker than others in the essay. While there is an attempt to focus this on recovery, with the use of the word 'revival', it really describes developments. Level 4 and above requires analytical responses, and so descriptive work such as this undermines the student's chances of achieving such a high level. While the information is potentially relevant, the student would need to organise this to support an argument and analysis that are firmly focused on the question. This improvement could come by first deciding on criteria by which 'recovery' could be measured.

this period. Production actually declined in 1926 and unemployment was always above 1.3 million. Additionally, Germany suffered from significant industrial disputes. The arbitration measures that the Weimar Coalition introduced were intended for emergencies, but they were made use of 76 000 times in the period of 1924–32. Some groups were also not successful economically during this period. Farmers, shopkeepers and many white-collar workers saw their incomes fall, relative to the growing wages of industrial workers. Many of these groups went on to support Hitler from 1929 as they felt their way of life had been undermined by the supposed recovery of this period.

The impact of Germany's foreign policy successes on domestic policies was significant, contributing to a recovery and thus political stability. The signing of the Locarno Treaty in 1925, peacefully accepting the western borders agreed at the Treaty of Versailles, saw Germany's relations with other nations rehabilitated to a considerable degree, leading to Germany joining the League of Nations in 1926. Stresemann was largely responsible for these efforts, which were welcomed by the vast majority of Germans as a policy of peaceful revision of the harsh terms imposed at Versailles. Although some nationalists were dissatisfied by these, they were in the minority, with the DNVP support for democracy during this period being a success. Additionally, these produced real gains for Germany, such as the financial support of the Dawes Plan and the later Young Plan of 1929, as well as a reduction in the Rhineland occupation forces by 10 000 in 1927. Although it is clear these arrangements were not strong enough to survive the test of the 1930s, within the years of 1924–9, it was undoubtedly a major part of the recovery, bringing political stability by increasing electoral support for the moderate coalition parties.

Thus the period of 1924–9 has to be seen as one of political stability and genuine recovery, even if this was only temporary. The leaders of Germany in these years made considerable progress when compared to their predecessors, and while they didn't form fully stable coalitions or eliminate the threat from extremist parties that re-emerged after 1929, the economic growth, cultural revival and successes in foreign policy were significant.

The student now moves on to the issue of the economy. Valid points are made regarding the lack of a recovery, with some attempt to analyse this. A good range of issues are covered in one paragraph, with strong specific supporting detail. However, it lacks a convincing argument and, towards the end, is really just describing economic problems. In order to improve, the paragraph should be structured more around focused arguments – recovery/not recovery – ideally exploring and weighing up how far the progress of the economy during this period reveals whether there was or was not a genuine recovery.

This penultimate paragraph is one of the stronger parts of the essay. It starts with a focused argument that links recovery and stability. Good knowledge of the issues is used to develop points and, although this could be more clearly focused on examining the extent of the recovery, a valid judgement is given that links to the question.

The conclusion does offer a well-focused judgement. There is reasoning to support the decision that has been made and, while this is relatively brief, it does draw together most of the issues from the main part of the essay. However, it lacks depth. The paragraph would benefit from weighing up the judgements that have been made to reach an overall decision on the question, which relates to both stability and recovery.

This is a moderate answer that contains the qualities of a high level 3 response:

- It is broadly analytical, showing an understanding of the focus of the question of stability and recovery.
- Some of the material included is descriptive or only implicitly relevant, such as the detail on cultural issues.
- Accurate and relevant evidence is given, but this is not always used to develop an analysis or reach judgements, such as the detail on economic issues.
- It is high in the level due to the good range of points across both of the issues of political stability and recovery, with a sufficient depth of knowledge to lift the answer within the level.
- The argument shows some direction and control but is not sustained on an assessment of the extent to which political stability and a genuine recovery were seen.

Overall, this answer would achieve **high level 3 and 18 marks**.

Grade A* student answer

The period of 1924 to 1929 did see a recovery in Germany to some extent, certainly when compared with the turmoil that came after. However, the extent to which this was genuine and stable is questionable. While in economic terms there was an overall recovery and no significant negative events, such as were seen before or afterwards with hyperinflation and the onset of the depression from 1929 onwards, this was both artificial and vulnerable in the sense it relied on overseas loans. Similarly, while the political system appeared more stable, with fewer elections being required and less of a threat from extremism, it is hard to consider this stable, with shifting coalitions and little sign that parties were maturing beyond interest groups to be capable of sustaining a successful democracy over the longer term.

In political terms there was a sense of stability, at least relative to the periods before and after. The lack of significant extra-parliamentary threat after the defeat of the Beer Hall *Putsch* and a dramatic reduction in political murders since 1922 must be seen to be a success. While combat leagues did develop on both sides of the political spectrum, these were marginal and of little threat to stability, with clashes between these only starting to ☞

This excellent introduction sets out a range of issues that are clearly related to the argument in the question. While still keeping this relatively brief, the student manages to establish provisional arguments and judgements that show a clear understanding of a range of issues that relate to both stability and recovery, and an ability to balance and weigh points critically. The answer shows confident and critical argument from the very start, which creates a very good impression and shows the potential to fulfil the level 5 criteria of sustaining analysis.

In this paragraph the student establishes a criterion for assessing stability by using the periods before and after as a 'benchmark' against which to measure stability. Own knowledge is sufficiently detailed, well selected and, more importantly, used to further the argument and examine the extent to which there was stability in terms of the extra-parliamentary threat to the Republic. The paragraph finishes with a clear evaluation of the stability that was displayed in light of the criterion of extra-parliamentary threat – relative to the preceding period.

grow from 1928 onwards. However, the absence of such negatives was not in itself a sign of real political stability, rather what Kolb described as 'relative stability'; it gave the Weimar Republic the chance to concentrate on establishing genuine democratic roots, but can only be seen as a qualified success in that it had recovered from the traumatic year of 1923.

When viewed from the perspective of the time, the experience of parliamentary democracy in the Reichstag appeared to offer a cautious optimism for the stability and potential long-term success of democracy. Extreme parties on both sides lost their share of the votes, with the KPD down to 9% by 1928 from a combined communist peak of 20% in 1920 while, on the extreme right, the Nazis vote over halved in the two elections of 1924, from 6.5% in May and were not significant again until the 1930 election. However, while there was support for democratic parties, this did not translate to stable government. Proportional representation was never likely to produce single-party rule, but the deeper problem was the failure of parties to mature to create stability within the system. Most parties still acted as interest groups, partly a legacy of the Second Reich, and were unable to act with a sufficient 'spirit of compromise' necessary to make coalitions work. Even in these relatively peaceful years, there were seven different governments in the period 1924–30, the longest of which lasted 21 months. These issues significantly undermined political stability as the predominantly minority coalitions failed to command effective government, agreeing more on foreign policy than domestic issues, and were easily collapsed by changes in party leadership or when faced with difficult issues. While the problems they had to contend with were by no means on the scale of later issues, they were by no means stable, and even before 1930, political legitimacy was being lost, particularly in the eyes of the crucial middle classes.

The period did also see a recovery in economic terms, although the extent of this is questionable as it was vulnerable to external shocks and ultimately brought down with the depression. Alongside the stabilisation of the currency with the *Rentenmark,* the Dawes Plan of 1924 brought a more realistic settlement on reparations and a loan of 800 million gold marks. The recovery as a result of this appeared remarkable; Stolper saw ☞

This paragraph is a more extended and developed point. The student offers extensive own knowledge, confidently applied to explore genuinely the issue of parliamentary stability. Clear emphasis is placed on the crucial issues, such as with 'the deeper problem was the failure of …'.

Although this is a longer than usual paragraph, it is effective in covering a range of issues without losing focus or analytical structure. There is clear argument throughout and reasoned evaluation is given at the end.

It is worth noting how the student highlights issues beyond 1929. Care must be taken over points like this, as the date range is only up to 1929. Some students underperform because they fail to focus carefully on the exact dates in a question. Here, the student briefly and effectively refers to the period after this to qualify their point, but this is perfectly acceptable, as the focus is firmly on the date range from the question.

this as 'unparalleled in recent German history'. Output levels for heavy industries and coal, iron and steel equalled and in cases surpassed pre-WWI levels. In one sense the recovery was genuine, productivity increased through improved technology and efficiency. However, although the higher wages and the generous social welfare benefits supported by the Weimar coalitions gave a sense of recovery and certainly benefited ordinary Germans, these were unsustainable – a burden the fragile recovery struggled to bear even with the US loans it was dependent upon. Production actually declined in 1926, with declining exports and unemployment never falling below 1.3 million. Industrial disputes such as the huge lockout at the Ruhr ironworks in 1928 disrupted production and limited the competitiveness of German producers. Such problems were merely masked by the high level of foreign investment. Thus, while there were elements of a genuine recovery, the reliance upon US loans left the economy vulnerable. The weaknesses were evident before 1929 and, with US investment being withdrawn from 1928, in economic terms the recovery should not be overstated.

Increased political stability, due to the impact of Germany's rehabilitation in foreign relations, was also evident. However, as with the increased foreign investment that brought economic recovery, the permanence of this is questionable. Along with the Dawes Plan, the signing of the Locarno Treaty in 1925 saw Germany's relations with other nations rehabilitated to a considerable degree, leading to Germany joining the League of Nations in 1926. While these measures provoked anger among nationalists, Stresemann's efforts were welcomed by most, seeing the DNVP move to supporting coalition government, and produced real gains for Germany, such as the financial support of the Dawes Plan and a reduction in the Rhineland occupation forces in 1927, with full withdrawal in 1929. The recovery this investment brought was undoubted, with over 25 billion marks stimulating economic output and higher wages. In cultural terms, Weimar Germany increasingly gained a reputation as a place of toleration and creativity, from Bauhaus architecture to the modernity of *Neue Sachlichkeit* in literature and theatre. The extent to which either of these developments constitutes a genuine recovery is a different matter. The latter was somewhat a departure of the more conservative culture of the ☞

Now the student moves on to economic issues, examining the extent to which there was a recovery. The paragraph is argued throughout, again using own knowledge to drive the argument forward rather than just to support points. There is clear analysis that weighs how far the various economic issues considered amount to a genuine recovery.

It is worth noting how the student discriminates within the time period in the question, essentially by emphasising how the recovery was greater in the first four years of the period, then started to fail from 1928. When faced with questions that only cover a short period of time, some students can fall into the trap of treating the period as one 'block' of time. Wherever possible and relevant, it will improve answers if you can highlight variation across a period.

Here the student examines other ways in which there was a recovery. Although somewhat unusual, it is structured effectively to cover foreign policy and cultural issues together. While the exam doesn't expect you to write about foreign policy in detail, the domestic impact of foreign policy is required, which is what is considered here.

It is worth comparing the treatment of cultural issues with the Grade C answer. Consider the difference in how the material is made relevant and argued effectively.

Second Reich, but these cultural developments really highlight the division in Germany. There was a reaction against the cultural freedom among more conservative elements of German society and, while this didn't stop this being a recovery of sort, it emphasises the more fundamental divisions that were not healing during this period. Perhaps more significantly, while the domestic benefits resulting from foreign policy, both in terms of real economic gains, as well as the improved public optimism towards Germany's prospects under democratic government shown by the reduced attraction of extreme parties, was one of the greatest successes of the period, Stresemann's methods of revision through fulfilment were a work in progress. He himself felt by 1929 this was beginning to disappoint, and certainly was not successfully embedded enough to survive the more testing circumstances that came after, and thus the implications of this for Germany cannot be seen as a recovery with long-term prospects.

Thus the period of 1924–9 cannot be seen as one of political stability and genuine recovery. While a recovery of sorts did take place, with significant economic growth, this was reliant upon external support, and while this hadn't failed by 1929, the gains made were already being eroded. As far as political stability was concerned, in relative terms the period was a success. However, this was in part dependent upon a recovery in areas such as the economy and foreign policy, which were themselves fragile. Thus, while the Weimar Republic was under less threat and the functioning of government was broadly smooth, this had failed to mature in a way that would have prepared it to deal with the problems that came later, and was increasingly losing legitimacy even before 1929 and so cannot be seen as a genuine recovery.

Even the fairly straightforward emphasis of 'Perhaps more significantly' adds to the answer, prioritising arguments.

As with previous paragraphs, this is well-structured and reaches a clear and reasoned overall judgement.

The overall conclusion clearly flows from the analysis and evaluation that have been offered throughout the answer. The student effectively draws together and weighs the different strands of argument on both political stability and recovery. They reach a critical judgement that effectively examines a range of themes across Weimar politics, economics and culture, both on an individual basis and collectively, exploring the links between these. The conclusion maintains the sharp focus, with a well-reasoned overall judgement that clearly links back to criteria – permanence and relativity – established from the introduction.

This is an excellent answer. All the qualities of a high level 5 response are present.

It has a focused and sustained analysis culminating in an explicit judgement on the extent to which there was stability and a recovery. There is consistent use of accurate and relevant evidence to support the analysis and evaluation. It is by no means a perfect answer – for example, it could go further in exploring the interplay between the issues of stability and recovery. However, it does address both of these issues as distinct points, something that is crucial when faced with a question that has two issues for judgement.

Overall, this answer would achieve **level 5 and gain the full 30 marks**.

Section A: essay question

'During the period 1939–45, opponents within the army posed a greater threat to Hitler and the Nazi regime than any other opposition group.'
How far do you agree with this statement? **[30 marks]**

This question requires you to make and justify an historical judgement about the extent to which the opposition from within the army posed a greater threat than other opposition groups during the war years. An examiner will be looking for:

1. an analytical (not a descriptive) response that focuses on opposition to the Nazi regime, with relevant supporting evidence drawn from across the 1939–45 timeframe
2. an informed assessment of the threat posed by both 'opponents within the army' *and* 'other opposition groups'
3. a substantiated judgement that supports or challenges the statement in the question.

Grade C student answer

Although the Nazis had made extensive use of the *Gestapo*, People's Courts, the SA and SS to repress and remove opposition, it did exist in various forms during the Second World War. As well as opposition from within the army, ideological opponents from the left continued, while the Church was also a source of opposition over particular moral issues. As well as this, disaffection among youths at times became genuine opposition, and sections of the conservative elites did form links with other opposition groups, and much of this opposition grew as the war turned against Germany. That said, the army was the only group that had the strength, size and access to the regime to pose a real threat.

At the start of the period in 1939, opposition from within the army, including Franz Halder, the Head of the General Staff, and Wilhelm Canaris, the Head of the *Abwehr*, planned to threaten the regime, aiming to prevent war. However, as with earlier plans from 1938, the planned coup was aborted. This was partly down to many officers being *Junkers* with anti-Polish sentiments. Although discussion of removing Hitler had abounded in high ranks for years, continuing throughout the war, these were never betrayed to the *Gestapo*. The army had ☞

This is a somewhat limited introduction. Although the issues outlined are substantially relevant to the question, they are introduced in a descriptive form. It is only really in the final sentence that a link is made to what the question has asked the student to do. In order to improve the quality of this, you would aim to briefly set out clear arguments regarding the levels of threat that different forms of opposition posed to the regime.

The student displays good knowledge regarding early opposition from within the ranks of the army. While a little descriptive to begin with, the student does develop into an examination of the threat. This is a little provisional though; the student outlines a strength and then a weakness (as a threat), but does not fully use this knowledge to assess the level of threat and reach a judgement. Additionally, the paragraph could be improved by starting with a more focused argument.

strength as a potential threat to the regime, with close-knit ranks unlikely to betray plotters. However, you can also see the conservative nature of the army, meaning it was in the main unwilling to lead a coup against an authority they had sworn an oath of loyalty to.

Failures in wartime meant growing criticism among the officer ranks, questioning Hitler's decision-making, and also justifying a potential coup in terms of the needs of the country. In the period 1943–4, there were at least six planned attempts on Hitler's life by serving military officers. Such an assassination threat was always the most likely way of toppling the regime, or at least the crucial figurehead. As wartime failure increased the suspicion of the *Gestapo* towards army plots, Hitler's protection was increased accordingly. The Stauffenberg bomb plot of 1944 was the high point of these attempts. During the summer of 1944, conspirators within the army had opened up negotiations with British and American diplomats. In July 1944, Stauffenberg, a devout Catholic with leanings towards social democracy, had become involved with the Beck–Goereler group. As a high-ranking member of the General Staff, Stauffenberg was able to leave a bomb in a suitcase at a meeting Hitler was attending at his miltary headquarters in Rastenburg. That it was only luck that Hitler escaped with minor injuries shows the potential threat opposition from within the army posed to the Nazis.

Again, the response is somewhat descriptive. Analysis is present to some degree, but this is mostly implicit. In such a way, a student who is clearly knowledgeable is likely to underperform by not fully and explicitly directing the argument towards the question. A stronger approach would be to plan a paragraph around arguments for and against, organising the information as follows: make the argument that the army was a threat in the period of 1943–4; make points to counter this; finally weigh up the points made with a judgement.

The Church was special in the sense that it was the one belief system and social organisation that was allowed to exist as a potential rival to the beliefs of the Nazis. Within the Catholic Church, to whom the concordat offered greater protection, there were instances of outspoken opposition. Bavarian Catholics were successful in having *Gauleiter* Wagner's ban on crucifixes in schools overturned in 1941, and von Galen's outspoken attack from the pulpit meant the Aktion T-4 programme was stepped down, if not ended. However, these were one-offs and the Church never fundamentally challenged the regime. Additionally, it served to support the regime in its crusade against communism and condemned the bomb plot in 1944, and thus failed to mobilise its mass support into being real opposition. Although notable exceptions were similarly found in the Protestant Church, such as Bonhoeffer's arrest and later execution for involvement in assassination attempts, or Niemoller's actions, they were too fragmented to pose any real threat. ☞

The starter sentence in this paragraph is broadly directed at the question. As the argument develops, specific knowledge is increasingly used more effectively, examining the extent of the threat. While the judgement could be more effectively developed by weighing against other relevant points (for example, 'Was the Church more/less of a threat than the army? Was it just a different kind of threat?'), it is a stronger paragraph than previous ones because it is more focused on discussing the question. Even so, a more confident opening sentence, which tackles the question, could still be used to improve this paragraph.

The chance of serious threat from the left was fundamentally weakened by the Nazi repression of political opponents from 1933 onwards. That said, the left did still show sizeable resistance during the war. There were 89 communist cells in Berlin alone in 1941 and, although these were hampered by the Nazi–Soviet Pact in the early years, they were more organised under the leadership of Wilhelm Knochel from 1942, with Soviet support. However, the *Gestapo* was often successful in infiltrating even small cells, and their greatest successes probably amounted to sabotage on wartime production lines, which, while they may have disrupted the war effort, cannot be seen as a real threat. Ex-SPD members, who were also increasingly disillusioned with their exiled leadership, formed splinter groups such as Red Patrol and Socialist Front.

The student starts with a clear point relating to the level of threat posed by the left. This is developed with specific knowledge, with clear discussion of the issue in the question. The most obvious way to improve this paragraph would be by developing a clear judgement, weighing up the extent to which the left posed a threat. Again, if relevant, it can be effective to compare the level of threat to another point, such as the threat from within the army.

Opposition to the Nazis was also found in other sections of German society, in particular among the youth. Of those that actively sought to oppose the Nazis, the Eidelweiss Pirates were the largest and most organised, centred on working-class areas of the Rhineland. The rebellion displayed was through non-conformity, attacking Hitler Youth groups and even assisting in the resistance efforts of army deserters. In December 1942, over 700 members were arrested and many of these were publicly executed as a warning to others. The protest by the White Rose Movement in 1943 sparked the first major public demonstration against Hitler's rule in a decade, with university students marching through Munich. However, they were quickly repressed by the Nazis, with Hans and Sophie Scholl being sentenced to death by a People's Court.

Here the student moves on to the issue of opposition from youth groups. Good understanding and knowledge are displayed. However, the answer has drifted back to describing what youth groups did, and so it is only implicitly dealing with the question.

Inconsistency of this kind, with a mix of strong paragraphs and weak paragraphs, are typical of level 3 answers. This is why carefully reading a question and planning an answer can make such a difference, ensuring you make the very best of the knowledge you take into an exam.

As far as the elites were concerned, groups such as Carl Goerdeler and his acquaintances, or the Kriesau Circle, can be seen as offering some opposition. The Kriesau Circle was effectively a dinner-party group whose elite status afforded them a position to meet and criticise the regime. Certain figures from the Kriesau Circle, such as Adam von Trott zu Solz, were linked to the Stauffenberg Bomb Plot. Similarly, Goerdeler's group had links across the civil service and military, such as General Beck, and did attempt to build links with the Allies. As with the Kriesau Circle, the involvement of some members with the bomb plot meant they were easily investigated and punished. Therefore, the extent of the threat that the conservative elites posed can be likened to the army. ☞

Again, this is an implicit paragraph. For example, the comment concerning the Kriesau Circle – that they were 'effectively a dinner-party group' – is potentially very good, highlighting that the nature of their opposition was polite talk, which did not set out to attack the Nazi regime. However, the student does not explicitly make this argument.

In the final sentence, a judgement is attempted, but this is limited as it is not explained. A better judgement would be reasoned – in this case, clearly exploring the way in which the extent of the threat of the elites could be said to be similar to that posed by the army.

In conclusion, the most ideologically motivated group of opponents were those from the left, although they were severely weakened by 1939 and so were unable to offer up any real threat. Church groups were awkward for the Nazis to deal with, but they did not act as a coherent threat. Youth protest had enthusiasm and bravery, but had little strength to really oppose the regime effectively. The army could have been the strongest threat, but it was only small sections of this that actually attempted to put into action their dislike of the regime as, due to their conservative nature and oath of loyalty, they were reluctant to oppose the Nazis.

This is a valid conclusion, as far as it goes. In the main, it briefly sums up the threat from different groups, then offers a rather indecisive judgement about the army. What the conclusion should really do is answer the question – judgements on each individual group should have been dealt with already. A better conclusion would at least attempt to weigh up the *relative* threat of different groups and provide an answer, explaining the evaluation given.

This is a moderate answer that contains the qualities of a high level 3 response:

- It is broadly analytical, showing an overall understanding of the focus of the question on threats to the regime.
- Accurate and relevant evidence is given, but this is not always used to develop an analysis or reach judgements, with sections on youth and elite opposition offering strong knowledge that is not fully directed at the question.
- The good range of points on both opposition from within the army and other opposition groups and the depth of own knowledge are sufficient to lift the answer high within the level.
- The material is almost always relevant and broadly discusses the issue in the question, but the focus on the question and so the assessment of the extent of the threat is often left implicit.

Overall, this answer would achieve **level 3 and 18 marks**.

Grade A student answer

While the Nazi regime appeared dominant in the early years of the war, as they had beforehand, with no effective opposition, threats did exist and in many ways grew as the early successes of the war stalled and were ultimately reversed. The army did offer the greatest potential for a realistic threat, in terms of organisation, force and proximity to the regime, and thus growing dissatisfaction within the army was significant, particularly when considered against the fragmented nature of other opposition groups, such as those on the left or dissenting youth groups, or the largely mild opposition that stemmed from the Churches.

Opposition from within the army potentially posed a significant threat from the very start of the war in 1939. Leading officers, including Franz Halder, the Head of the General Staff, planned to threaten the regime, aiming to prevent war. However, as with earlier plans from 1938, the planned coup was aborted. While this was partly down to many officers being *Junkers* with anti-Polish sentiments, it highlights the limitations of the army as a threat. On the one hand, although discussion of removing Hitler had abounded in high ranks for years, continuing throughout the war, these were never betrayed to the *Gestapo*, reflecting the close ranks and strength of the officer corps. On the other, it reveals how it was not in the conservative nature of the army to lead a coup against an authority to which they had sworn an oath of loyalty, even when many believed the regime was both ideologically and strategically at odds with the interests of the Reich.

Where the threat of the army can be seen to have grown is from 1943 onwards, as failures in wartime meant many more within the officer ranks questioned Hitler's strategic leadership. In the period 1943–4, there were at least six planned attempts on Hitler's life by serving military officers, including the failed timed device planted on Hitler's flight to Rastenburg. While these all ultimately failed, it offered the most realistic chance of toppling Hitler, as the army had the autonomy, means and opportunity to pose a realistic assassination threat. However, as wartime failure increased the suspicion of the *Gestapo* towards army plots, Hitler's protection was increased accordingly. The Stauffenberg bomb plot was in this sense a last realistic attempt; it was only by fortune that Hitler survived, and so in terms of Hitler personally it was the greatest threat. 👉

This relatively brief yet strong introduction confidently sets out a clear grasp of the demands of the question. While it only briefly touches on the other issues to be examined, it offers clear argument regarding the nature and extent of the threat posed by both the army and other groups, and thus gives a provisional judgement that indicates what is to be examined.

The student displays a clear understanding and knowledge of the nature and extent of the threat that the army posed in the early years. In a straightforward yet effective way, the student sets out argument and counter-argument ('On the one hand … on the other …'), offering a clear analytical focus. The paragraph would benefit from a more developed evaluation, reaching a judgement about the extent of the threat at this point.

The answer is clearly focused, beginning with a reasoned argument. A particular strength here is the way in which the changing extent of the threat is emphasised, as even though the question only deals with a six-year period, the extent of the threat did vary. This point is developed through the paragraph. Supporting knowledge is good and effectively deployed. Judgements are offered, although these would be improved by developing the final sentence; for example, a critical distinction could be made over the extent to which toppling the Führer amounted to the same as a threat to the regime. Even if the answer to this was 'yes', it would highlight the subtleties of the question.

In a similar manner to the army, other opposition groups all were limited in their capacity to threaten the regime. In one sense, the Church held a certain level of protection in that it was the one alternative belief system allowed to exist within the regime without being systematically purged, and so the existence of such a powerful social organisation outside Nazi *Gleichschaltung* gave it a status from which it could potentially threaten the regime. However, even the Catholics, for whom the 'concordat' offered greater protection, were not beyond reach when they did criticise. Although Bavarian Catholics were successful in having *Gauleiter* Wagner's ban on crucifixes in schools overturned in 1941, and von Galen's outspoken attack from the pulpit meant the Aktion T-4 programme was stepped down, if not ended, these were notable exceptions. The Church afforded its members some protection and was certainly a bulwark against the totalitarian intent of the regime, but it only really challenged the regime on selective moral issues that did not fundamentally threaten Nazi authority. Thus, it cannot be seen as a real threat as, when members of the Church did oppose the regime, their protected status was lost.

The most obvious opposition to the Nazis, that from the left, in the sense that they were had politically stood in direct contrast to Nazi values, were fundamentally weakened for this very reason, as their forthright opposition had made them a target for being closed down by Nazi repression. Nazi measures against their political opponents had reduced them to a shattered rump that, during wartime, offered little realistic chance of organised revolt. While there were 89 communist cells in Berlin alone in 1941, they were hampered by the Nazi–Soviet Pact in the early years, and although somewhat rallied under the leadership of Wilhelm Knochel from 1942, with Soviet support, they were easily infiltrated, as shown by Knochel's own conviction in 1944. The divided nature of the left was also a weakness. Ex-SPD members, increasingly disillusioned with their exiled leadership, formed splinter groups such as the Red Patrol and Socialist Front. While these were more assertive and did attempt to cooperate with other groups, they were far from unified and had little impact on the regime.

Opposition to the Nazis was also found in other sections of German society, in particular among the youth. While much of this was more disaffection or disdain for Nazi beliefs and values, with little by the way of organised attempts to actively oppose the regime, some ☞

A clear argument is given, with some attempt to relate the nature and level of threat to that of the stated issue – opposition from within the army. However, this is not fully developed.

It is worth comparing this paragraph to the parallel paragraph in the Grade C answer (page 124). While the Grade C answer actually covers more supporting knowledge than this, which only really looks at the Catholic Church, it is used less effectively. The strength of this paragraph is that it clearly argues and gives a reasoned evaluation about the nature, and thus extent, of the threat the Church posed to the regime.

Another a well-organised paragraph that makes good use of the material it covers. It clearly argues that the left was not a great threat, explaining the point with selected own knowledge. The paragraph is complete, with an effective judgement that offers clear critieria on which to base a focused assessment.

groups that can be considered as threatening did emerge from these. The Eidelweiss Pirates were the most organised of the youth groups. Centred on working-class areas of the Rhineland, the rebellion among these street gangs was seen as threatening in terms of the potential it had to spread disaffection. That the Nazis were able to contain their activities easily, arresting over 700 members in December 1942, executing many of these publicly as a warning to others, highlights their lack of real threat.

In conclusion, the army can be seen to have been the greatest threat to the regime, insofar as it was opposition from within this group that came the closest to actually killing Hitler. However, such a judgement is marginal; assassination attempts aside, all of these groups struggled to offer effective opposition, as the opportunity for organised resistance was limited by the authorities. The left and youth opposition was arguably the most motivated, but their limited resources and fractured groups could only offer sporadic resistance, while the Churches had widespread support and were hard for even the Nazis to close down, but as institutions they did not really attempt to threaten the regime.

The final main point considers youth opposition. The nature of the threat is considered and the activities of the Eidelweiss Pirates are discussed. The paragraph lacks the real depth of analysis needed for level 5, but material is directed at the question and a valid judgement is explained.

This is an effective conclusion, with a clear judgement that weighs different issues, to some degree. The answer could have made more of this here, as it could have done throughout the main points; for instance, astute comments regarding the nature of the threat offered opportunities for critical evaluation (for example, exploring and reaching judgement on what exactly constituted a threat to the Nazis). Similarly, the answer would have benefited from more consistent weighing-up of points to evaluate the relative threat posed by different groups throughout the answer.

This is a good answer, displaying the qualities of a high level 4 response:

- It is focused and analytical, clearly considering the relative level of threat posed by the different opposition groups.
- It demonstrates understanding of key issues, such as the nature of the opposition groups and what constituted a threat, with some evaluation of argument.
- There is consistent use of accurate and relevant evidence on the different opposition groups to support the analysis, with well-chosen and specific knowledge on the left, youth and Church as well as opposition within the army.
- It is by no means a perfect answer: for example, at times judgements are not fully developed to examine the relative threat of different groups, and it is relatively brief compared to some that may be seen. Nevertheless, it achieves a high level 4 as it is secure in demonstrating the skills required.

It is also worth noting, in comparison to the Grade C answer, that fewer points are actually considered. This answer does not look at the conservative elites. What makes this a stronger response, nevertheless, is its more consistent focus on argument and analysis.

Overall, this answer would achieve **level 4 and 23 marks**.

- -

Section B: controversy question

Use Sources 1, 2 and 3 and your own knowledge.

How far do you agree with the view that Germany's aggressive actions were chiefly responsible for the outbreak of the First World War?

Explain your answer using the evidence of Sources 1, 2 and 3 and your own knowledge of the issues related to this controversy.   **[40 marks]**

Source 1

(From David Blackbourn, *History of Germany 1780–1918*, published by Blackwell Publishing 2002)

German responsibility for war should not be restricted to the issue of whether Bethmann, or the German government, or the Kaiser, desired peace in 1912–14 or, for that matter, earlier. Of course they would have preferred to get what they wanted without war. But German actions going back to the 1890s had done much to create international tension. Bethmann personally was a sensitive, passive, fatalistic man, but he was faced with reaping the whirlwind sown by his predecessors. Others bore more responsibility, like Tirpitz, who built a battle fleet aimed at the British but professed his peaceful intentions.

Source 2

(From L.F.C. Turner, *The Origins of the First World War*, published by W.W. Norton 1970)

After Sarajevo, Wilhelm II and Bethmann-Hollweg courted a great war and, in view of the prevailing mood in Paris and St Petersburg, there was little hope of averting catastrophe after the Austrian ultimatum was presented in Belgrade. The crisis got out of control because Bethmann pushed Austria into a premature declaration of war on Serbia. The French General Staff drove Russia along the fatal path to mobilization. This conduct reflected French confidence in victory, but was also a reaction to the German war plan devised by Count von Schlieffen. That plan, with its flagrant violations of neutrality, had been approved by the German Government since 1904. In the final phase, military considerations were of decisive importance.

Source 3

(From Niall Ferguson, *The Pity of War*, published by Allen Lane 1998)

The extent of German malice aforethought must not be exaggerated. For men who have been accused of planning a war, the senior members of the German General Staff were uncannily relaxed in July 1914. At the time the Kaiser issued his famous 'blank cheque' to the Austrians, Moltke, Waldersee, Groener, chief of the Railway Section, and Major Nicolai, the head of key intelligence agency Section 111b, were all on holiday (in separate resorts, it should be said). Tirpitz and Admiral von Pohl were too. It was only on 16th July that Nicolai's stand-in, Captain Kurt Neuhof, was advised to step up surveillance of Russian military activity. Nicolai himself was not back at his desk for another two days. Even then his orders to the so-called 'tension travellers' – i.e. German spies in Russia and France – were merely to find out 'whether war preparations are taking place in France and Russia'.

This controversy question requires you to make and justify an historical judgement about the extent to which Germany was responsible for the outbreak of the First World War. An examiner will be looking for:

1. an analytical response that focuses on the competing interpretations concerning the origins of the First World War and evaluates them
2. relevant supporting evidence drawn from the sources provided and your own knowledge
3. effective cross-referencing of the source material to develop a support/challenge approach
4. effective integration of the source material and your own knowledge
5. a conclusion containing a substantiated judgement that supports or challenges the statement in the question.

Grade C student answer

Germany's aggressive actions can be identified as a cause of the First World War, with a foreign policy that from the 1890s onwards created tension with France and Britain over colonial, naval and European security issues. Germany has also been argued to have been deeply responsible in terms of its actions during the crisis of July 1914, by offering unlimited support to Austro–Hungary through the 'blank cheque', which can be seen to have escalated the Balkan conflict into a general European war. However, while some historians point to detailed planning for war, others argue Germany was as much a victim of circumstances as the other European nations. The alliance system, which locked nations in and impacted upon their plans for mobilisation, was as much the responsibility of the *Entente* nations, while the response of the Austrian leaders and even the Russian Tsar after the shooting of the Archduke Franz Ferdinand can equally be blamed. In Source 1, Blackbourn looks at the actions of German leaders.

In Source 1, Blackbourn raises the argument that German leaders from the 1890s onwards were responsible as they 'had done much to create international tension', with the likes of Tirpitz having developed naval plans which increased tension through challenging the British. This is partly supported by Turner (Source 2), who highlights the approval of Schlieffen's plan by the German government despite the 'flagrant violations of neutrality' it involved. German leaders from the 1890s onwards did undertake actions that can be seen as aggressive. In fact, even before this time, Britain and Germany had clashed over interests in east Africa, although these stayed localised and were settled by peaceful negotiation. Britain also clashed with France over Fashoda in 1898. Such disputes rarely spilled over into European problems, although they did contribute to Britain's diplomatic isolation. Negotiations between Britain and Germany even took place from 1898 to come to an Anglo–German understanding, so war was by no means inevitable from this time. However, the increasing threat that Germany's naval plans, encouraged under von Bülow's belief that *Flottenpolitik* could be used to build a navy that Britain could not ignore and that would gain Germany colonial concessions, can be seen as aggressive. This backfired, as it never seriously threatened British naval supremacy, but it did end the chances of an Anglo–German understanding and led to Britain and France putting aside their differences. This in turn ☞

If the student were answering a Section A essay question, this would be a very strong introduction. It has a clear focus on the specific demands of the question, clearly establishing a range of arguments and issues, and demonstrating a confident knowledge of the historical debate surrounding the origins of the First World War. It also begins to offer a provisional judgement, indicating a direction of argument it will follow, while leaving issues sufficiently open to allow a balanced discussion.

However, Section B answers require a different approach. With the exception of the weak final sentence, this answer barely acknowledges that the debate is centred on the three given extracts. In order to improve, the student should frame the introduction to the debate about the key issues and arguments raised in the three sources.

This first main paragraph of the essay showcases the following potential strengths:

- a clear ability to interpret the key arguments within the sources, making good reference to Sources 1 and 2
- an ability to link and cross-reference these sources
- excellent own knowledge of the long-term issues behind the outbreak of the First World War
- an ability to apply this own knowledge to developing argument and analysis, explaining developments and reasoning over the importance of different issues.

However, this is not put together effectively. The student raises valid issues from Sources 1 and 2, which should be explored further, but instead they extend this in a way that starts to drift from the central issues to events which, while relevant to some degree, are away from the focus of the point raised and the ideas in the sources. Additionally, the attempt at a judgement in the final sentence is essentially asserted, with limited reasoning to link this back to the preceding analysis. To improve this, the student should aim to integrate the sources and own knowledge more effectively, using specific knowledge to reach a judgement that is explained and firmly linked to the analysis that comes before it.

led to the *Entente* and then the Schlieffen Plan, which was developed as a response to the threat Germany had brought upon itself. Therefore the actions of German leaders were responsible for developments that led to the First World War.

The Schlieffen Plan can be blamed for causing the war, although how aggressive it was is more debatable. As Turner highlights, it came about as a result of concerns over Britain joining the *Entente* in 1904. In this manner, German leaders can be deemed as rash in their actions. The Schlieffen Plan may have been intended to be defensive, but it dominated Germany's actions thereafter, with Wilhelm accepting the advice of military advisers with little questioning. In this sense, while Turner argues Bethmann 'courted a great war', he was more the 'passive' character that Blackbourn portrays as 'reaping the whirlwind of his predecessors'. Bülow had done more to stir nationalism and create a policy of clumsy brinkmanship that did 'create' the 'international tension', Blackbourn considers. Schlieffen, the Chief of the General Staff from 1891, developed a plan in response to the Kaiser's shift in foreign policy, with the ending of the Reinsurance Treaty between Germany and Russia and the increasingly strong relations with Austria. Fearing a potential war with France and Russia, who had grown closer as a result of German support for Austro–Hungary during the Bulgarian Crisis of 1878, Schlieffen drew up a plan to deal with a war on both fronts. In order to defeat France quickly, before Germany was able to mobilise, the idea of a lightning strike through the Low Countries was developed, encircling but not taking Paris. This was accepted by Germany's leaders from 1904 (Source 2) and updated by Moltke after Schlieffen's death. So, the development and acceptance of the Schlieffen Plan by Germany's leaders must be seen as crucial, setting Germany against France and Britain and firming up war plans which increased tension.

Ferguson shows how the German generals were in a relaxed state during the July Crisis. He details how key decision-makers such as Moltke, Nicolai and Tirpitz were absent from Berlin on holiday while developments were unfolding. This is used to argue that German responsibility should 'not be exaggerated'. This stands in contrast with the view of Turner, who suggests that Wilhelm and Bethmann-Hollweg 'courted a great war' after the assassination in Sarajevo. While they are discussing different individuals, it is hard to see ☞

Here the cross-referencing of the two sources is stronger, relating their views to each other and developing an analysis from them. There is some integration with own knowledge although, again, there is a tendency to drift from points that have been raised in order to demonstrate details that have been remembered. The answer would be improved by careful selection of the most relevant points that could be used to further the debate. There is some attempt to offer a judgement that is focused on the question. However, this has not been fully reasoned, as the preceding information on the Schlieffen Plan is descriptive. Thus, while it may be correct that German leaders were responsible, the material is not used to provide a convincing analysis to support this.

The answer is focused and uses Sources 2 and 3 to develop some analysis. Valid points raised from the sources are discussed, showing understanding of key issues, and the student attempts to offer judgement on them. However, this paragraph lacks real depth of development – whereas previous paragraphs almost had too much own knowledge, which at times was losing relevance, here it is limited. To improve on this, use of specific own knowledge to substantiate the comments made should be applied. This would also make the judgement in the final sentence more convincing.

how key military planners would be allowed to be absent, as the Schlieffen Plan required Germany to act decisively if they thought France or Russia was due to mobilise.

Ferguson also highlights how German spies in France and Russia were 'merely' to find out if 'war preparations' were taking place, again suggesting that German responsibility was not evident from such actions. However, it can be argued that the 'merely' is all that was required, as the Schlieffen Plan meant that, should Russia mobilise against Germany, Germany would do so. As Turner indicates, at the same time Bethmann was putting pressure on Austria to declare war on Serbia, highlighting that Germany's plans were already in action. Although they may not have mobilised yet, in the hope that Russia may capitulate without going to war, they were in a position to do so. That said, as Turner suggests, the French themselves were pressuring Russia to mobilise in order that the *Entente* response to a possible attack under the Schlieffen Plan took place, so they must bear some responsibility for this as well.

German leadership must be seen to have been mainly responsible for the outbreak of the First World War, although there is evidence to suggest other factors contributed. The actions of other nations and the development of the alliances narrowed Germany's options. However, while many of the actions of German leaders were not intentionally aggressive, they contributed greatly to the tension that had developed in European diplomacy, and developed plans that meant both alliances were stood against each other in a situation where acting first was essential, but only made war more likely.

A further point is raised from Ferguson (Source 3). This is developed, considering the evidence of Source 2 and examining the merits of its arguments. However, while this is a potentially strong paragraph, it again shows a lack of depth. Detailed own knowledge and more of the sources should be used to make the commentary more convincing. This commentary could then be used to give a judgement linked to the question.

The conclusion offers a judgement in relation to the specific claim in the question. This is broadly supported by the attempts to analyse the sources and use own knowledge in the main body of the essay. To improve, the student could relate this more clearly to the views that have been discussed.

This answer demonstrates a good range of detailed own knowledge, such as the long-term problems and the development of the alliance system. However, at times it begins to drift, running the risk of dropping to level 3 ('broadly analytical'). Moreover, there is an imbalance, with extensive detail from own knowledge used in places and very little used in others. The answer is analytical, with an overall focus on issues and some good development, although argument and judgement are not always convincingly connected to the sources. The student is mainly confident in recognising the views in the given extracts, cross-referencing them and offering analysis of the different interpretations of German responsibility. There is some imbalance in the use of sources and integration is somewhat patchy.

This answer would achieve **level 4 and 11 marks for AO1a and b, level 4 and 15 marks for AO2b, and overall would gain 26 marks.**

Grade A* student answer

Collectively the sources offer a range of perspectives on the argument that the responsibility for the outbreak of the First World War should be chiefly placed with Germany's aggressive actions. Source 1 appears to most strongly support this view, with Blackbourn (Source 1) seeing responsibility in the actions of a range of German statesmen, particularly through the international tension they created from 1890. To an extent this is supported by Turner (Source 2), who highlights the effect of Germany's actions during the July Crisis of 1914, which were themselves a result of Schlieffen's war plan. Turner does, though, offer some mitigation for German responsibility, also seeing the attitude of the French and Russian governments and their response to developments in 1914. In contrast to Source 1, Ferguson suggests German responsibility was limited, focusing on their actions in July 1914 to suggest there was little evidence of an active desire to escalate matters.

Blackbourn's argument in Source 1, that German leaders from the 1890s onwards 'had done much to create international tension', with the likes of Tirpitz having developed naval plans that increased tension through challenging the British, is backed in part by Turner (Source 2), who highlights the approval of Schlieffen's plan by the German government despite the 'flagrant violations of neutrality' it involved. Ferguson (Source 3) does not entirely deny this, pointing to German observance of Russian and French military preparations, although the lack of urgency he highlights downplays the aggressive element. The issue of Belgian neutrality is perhaps overstated, as while the British declaration of war may have come on the violation of Belgian neutrality, the entanglements of the *Entente* were as much British concerns.

The Schlieffen Plan can be seen to have been significant, although not necessarily aggressive in intent, as the approval Turner points to was in itself a product of concerns over Britain joining the *Entente* in 1904. In this manner, German leaders can be deemed as rash in their actions. The Schlieffen Plan may have been intended to be defensive, but it dominated Germany's actions thereafter, with Wilhelm accepting the advice of military advisers with little questioning. In this sense, while Turner argues Bethmann 'courted a great war', he was more the 'passive' character that Blackbourn ☞

This strong introduction clearly sets out the main issues in the debate. These are focused on the specific demands of the question, using words from the question. The views of all three sources are set out, with clear emphasis of the position they take towards the question. To improve further, the introduction could offer a clear 'line of argument' – outline what is going to be argued – and even include a provisional judgement. This would be useful for setting out a path through the main points that will be examined, while also helping towards achieving level 5, which demands a 'sustained evaluative argument'.

In this relatively brief paragraph, the student manages to demonstrate the following skills:

- identifying and cross-referencing the views of all three sources
- offering a critical if not fully developed analysis of these
- using own knowledge to develop an analysis that begins to offer an evaluation, with some strong phrasing to suggest emphasis on the extent of agreement between interpretations, such as 'does not entirely deny this'.

To improve this further, the points could be developed in more depth, using more of the sources, such as Turner's reference to the French General Staff. They could also more clearly develop their attempts at evaluation to reach a judgement that is more specifically focused on the precise demands of the question, linking the issue of Belgium and *Entente* entanglements back to the given interpretation over the responsibility of 'Germany's aggressive actions'.

portrays as 'reaping the whirlwind of his predecessors'. Bülow had done more to stir pan-German sentiment and create a policy of clumsy brinkmanship, which did 'create' the 'international tension' Blackbourn considers, with Tirpitz's actions being the greatest example of this. His naval strategy, aimed at forcing Britain to concentrate on home ports and so allow Germany greater opportunity to exploit colonial ambition, backfired insofar as it brought Britain's focus on Europe in a different way, leading to the *Entente* that German statesmen thought near impossible.

Ferguson makes the case that the actions of the German high command during the July Crisis do not suggest a leadership actively planning war, countering Fischer's argument that premeditation can be seen from the 1912 War Council. Ferguson offers evidence of a range of key German military staff being on holiday during the midst of the crisis, while German spies monitoring Russian and French activity were not at a manner of alert one would expect during such tension. However, this does not fully deny German responsibility. The necessary plans for German action in the event of war had been laid out in some detail well before the crisis. The events of the crisis also question this view. The Austrian request for support was sent on 4 July, with the response of a 'blank cheque' of support for Austria following soon after from the Kaiser, in consultation with Bethmann-Hollweg. Germany then awaited developments in terms of a French and Russian response, who did not meet until the 20 July. Although the French, mindful of German plans, may have encouraged – as Turner suggests – Russian mobilisation, Russia still sought negotiation, with the Tsar Nicholas asking Kaiser Wilhelm to restrain Austria at this stage. French responsibility is evident in encouraging Russian mobilisation, which many already knew would lead to war through the Schlieffen Plan, but it was this very plan that created the impetus in the French to require Russia to mobilise. It is valid to argue that, even at this stage, Germany hoped to gain by concession without war, but equally, in taking advantage of the crisis, Germany was willing to risk war to further its own aims, is compelling. Even if German leaders hoped, as Ritter claims, that the war could remain localised, they were at the very least prepared to take the gamble of wider European war in the hope that Austria's position could be strengthened and the Triple *Entente* may have been split. Thus, while Ferguson may be correct to see ☞

There is a greater depth of development here than in the previous paragraph. The student makes a focused and somewhat nuanced argument, highlighting the nature of the Schlieffen Plan as it relates to the question (that it may have been at fault, but not necessarily aggressive). Two of the sources are used, and there is analysis of their views and the evidence they give, using selected own knowledge. While there could be greater depth of analysis, this is an analytical response that confidently discusses the sources, integrating these with own knowledge. There is argument and some judgement although, to improve, this could be more explicitly directed at the specific demands of the question.

This penultimate paragraph is well-focused towards the question, using Source 3 to establish a counter-argument. This is explored using evidence from the sources, with strong use of specific own knowledge to examine the issues raised. The answer also relates these arguments to two historiographical viewpoints, drawing on knowledge of the debate from historians beyond the given extracts. While this is by no means a requirement, these viewpoints are used effectively – although briefly, they are used with confidence and are focused towards debating the issue.

Overall, the paragraph offers well-developed analysis and evaluation which, in many ways, is indicative of the highest levels. However, it would benefit from making more use of the sources as the extended own knowledge analysis that is offered risks losing sight somewhat of the need to explore the debate within the sources. That said, the integration of the views of Fischer and Ritter with knowledge of events and issues is a strength of this paragraph.

the behaviour of the military leaders as being casual, there is still sufficient evidence to suggest that the actions of the political leaders carry some responsibility particularly in the context of well-established longer-term military plans.

German leadership alone clearly cannot be held responsible for causing the First World War. The nature of European problems before 1914 makes it impossible either to definitively prove or to deny the responsibility of almost any of the alliance nations. British decision-makers could have altered the path of developments, while Turner usefully points to French actions that increased tension. However, while the evidence does not suggest German aggression expressly intended to start war, Germany's unique circumstances meant its leaders did 'court' war, particularly by a policy of *Weltpolitik* intended to develop naval and imperial strength, but which only served to cement opposing alliances, increase European tension and ultimately reduce German options to a point where war had become a risk worth taking.

A clearly focused judgement is offered here, which shows understanding of the issues raised from the given extracts and the debate over German responsibility more generally. The judgement is fairly well reasoned, and this is linked to the view of Source 2. This does show a high level of analytical understanding, but perhaps could be more directly linked to the analysis within the main body of the essay – issues such as the responsibility of British leaders and the role of the alliances are referred to in the conclusion, yet these are not fully explored in the main body of the essay.

Overall, this answer contains the qualities of a high level 4 response in both Assessment Objectives:

- It has a consistent analytical focus on the extent of German responsibility.
- There is confident interpretation and analysis of the sources, examining the different perspectives on German responsibility offered by the first two, and contrasting these with Ferguson.
- Own knowledge is used to examine the debate. It is, in the main, well selected, although it is not fully balanced, being more in depth in some places than others.
- The sources and own knowledge are largely well integrated, although some points are not fully developed and opportunities to make more of the given evidence are missed, such as the earlier paragraph on the responsibility of Germany's military leaders.
- The answer offers sufficient evaluation within the essay and in the final conclusion, although a direct evaluative focus on the question of 'Germany's aggressive actions', is not fully sustained.

This answer would achieve **level 4 and 13 marks for AO1a and b, level 4 and 19 marks for AO2b, and overall would gain 32 marks**.

Section B: controversy question

Use Sources 1, 2 and 3 and your own knowledge.
How far do you agree with the view that 'the regime intimidated Germans into agreement'?
Explain your answer, using Sources 1, 2 and 3 and your own knowledge of the issues related to this controversy.
[40 marks]

Source 1
(From Richard Evans, *The Third Reich in Power*, published by Penguin 2005)

The truth is that far from being levelled exclusively against small and despised minorities, the threat of arrest, prosecution and incarceration in increasingly brutal and violent conditions loomed over everyone in the Third Reich. The regime intimidated Germans into agreement, visiting a whole range of sanctions upon those who dared oppose it, and depriving them of their traditional social and cultural surroundings such as the pub or club or the voluntary association, above all where these could be seen as a potential source of resistance, as in the case of the Labour movement. Fear and terror were integral parts of the Nazis' armoury of political weapons from the very beginning. Everything that happened in the Third Reich took place in this pervasive atmosphere of fear and terror, which never slackened.

Source 2
(From Eric A. Johnson, *Nazi Terror*, published by Basic Books 1999)

Most Germans were not Nazis. Nor were they Jews, members of the Communist underground, or Jehovah's Witnesses. Most slept soundly, worked productively, and enjoyed their lives during the peacetime years of National Socialist rule. Why should they not have? The economy was improving, most were finding employment, and their country was regaining its pride and was still at peace. They knew that Jews, Communists, Socialists, and some religious activists suffered persecution. They could read about it in the daily newspapers. They knew that there was a strong police presence, an excess of laws placing limitations on personal freedom, and potential danger for those who refused to comply with Hitler's wishes. Many grumbled and complained privately, but most found little difficulty in conforming. Many, probably most, still believed that the police and the laws were there to protect them. Nazi terror posed no real threat to most ordinary Germans.

Source 3
(From Robert Gellately, *Backing Hitler*, published by Oxford University Press 2001)

Most people in Nazi Germany had no direct confrontation with the Gestapo, Kripo, or the concentration camps. Moreover, while they read many stories about the 'People's Court', rather few people attended its sessions. In other words, for most Germans, the coercive side of Hitler's dictatorship was created by what passed along by word of mouth, by what they read in the press, or heard on the radio. Historians have paid remarkably little attention to these representations, when in fact these played an important role in the dictatorship.

At every level, there was much popular support for the expanding missions of the new police and the camps, especially as the latter were presented in the media and elsewhere as boot-camps in which the state would confine both 'political criminals' and variously defined asocials, in order to subject them to 'work therapy'.

This controversy question requires you to make and justify an historical judgement about the extent to which consent for the Nazi regime was based upon intimidation. An examiner will be looking for:

1. an analytical (not a descriptive) response that focuses on the competing interpretations of Nazi control and popularity in the years 1933–9 and evaluates them
2. relevant supporting evidence drawn from the sources provided and your own knowledge
3. effective cross-referencing of the source material to develop a support/challenge approach
4. effective integration of the source material and your own knowledge
5. a conclusion containing a substantiated judgement that supports or challenges the statement in the question.

Grade C student answer

The sources do offer very different perspectives on how the Nazis controlled the German people. Evans (Source 1) clearly argues that brutality and terror were the source of Nazi control, detailing the sanctions that faced all Germans. Source 2 argues a very different case, suggesting that while persecution did exist, most Germans had little to fear from this, and that in fact they enjoyed improved circumstances in many ways. Source 3 similarly shows most Germans as not suffering at the hands of the police state, in fact welcoming the attack on groups who were portrayed as being enemies of the German state.

Source 1 suggests that intimidation 'loomed over everyone' through the threat of arrest and punishment. Similarly Source 2 and Source 3 accept the existence of such sanctions, highlighting 'a strong police presence' and camps 'in which the state confined "political criminals"'. Johnson argues that most Germans accepted the 'excess of laws' as they perceived them as being 'there to protect them'. Similarly Gellately, suggests that most Germans supported the 'new police' and perceived the camps to be 'boot-camps' for asocials. A huge level of popular support can be seen for the regime generally, with the plebiscites of 1936 and 1938 suggesting this to be so. Additionally, there was a genuine belief that the regime was rebuilding Germany's strength after the Depression for Germany in general, as seen by the successful donations to the Winter Relief schemes each year or that 10 million Germans had enjoyed a holiday due to the KdF by 1938. That the Nazi regime made such benefits available to ordinary Germans supports Johnson's view that most Germans accepted what the regime had to offer and saw the punishments as being aimed at those who were a threat to this. This is something that Gellately also highlights, showing that, far from being intimidated, most Germans supported punishments for those who required 'work therapy'.

What was crucial in controlling Germans generally was the all-encompassing power of the police state. The Emergency Power Decree of February 1933 may have legitimated the expanding SS–police authority under Himmler's control, but it was the arbitrary ability to arrest Germans that caused fear, with 162 000 being placed in 'protective custody' without trial during 1933–9. Although the number of *Gestapo* agents was ☞

This sound but basic introduction shows awareness that the three sources are interpretations that take different views on the debate, and it sets out their arguments briefly. But these arguments are not developed explicitly in relation to the question. In order to improve further, the answer could link these arguments more clearly to the question and offer its own provisional judgement on the extent to which intimidation was used to gain consent.

In this first main paragraph, the student does again recognise the different views of the sources, briefly cross-referencing all three with some well-chosen quotes. This is also extended with some specific own knowledge regarding popular measures to evidence consent. However, while this potentially suggests a higher-level answer, it is limited as the knowledge and analysis of the extracts are not fully connected together, with the student moving away from the point concerning intimidation towards one on popularity without clear reasoning. Moreover, the analysis is not fully directed at the specific demands of the question. To improve further, the student could develop the analysis to examine more clearly the relationship between intimidation and popularity, or deal with these separately. A clearer judgement that follows from the analysis and is linked to the question would also improve this.

This paragraph is again broadly analytical, with a focus on control. The information is specific, relevant and is discussing issues that relate to the question. However, in order to improve further, it needs to focus more clearly on the debate within the sources, as this is where the majority of the marks are available. A more clearly planned response, which identifies the arguments and issues from the extracts and combines them with use of the knowledge above, would score more highly. Additionally, a clear judgement on the issue would again improve the answer.

usually relatively small, compared to the population, with a city such as Dusseldorf, population 4 million, having only 281 agents, they did place great fear in the lives of ordinary Germans. People were aware that they were only a denunciation away from arrest, with over 80% of investigations arising this way.

In a way, the above point supports the view of Evans, that the threat of 'arrest, persecution and incarceration…' loomed over everyone', as few could be sure that such a denunciation wouldn't happen to them. However, it also shows the merits of Gellately's point in a way, as it highlights 'popular support' for these measures if so many people were willing to denounce others who they suspected of political crimes. Therefore, intimidation did exist, which played a role in gaining the agreement of ordinary Germans.

Although it has to be accepted that intimidation played a significant role, it is harder to determine the level of influence this had and on what proportion of Germans. Johnson's argument that most of the ordinary Germans who fitted the Nazi idea of the *volk* 'enjoyed their lives' under Nazi rule is convincing in this respect. Many were better off under the Nazis due to achievements such as the increased employment that Johnson highlights and, in this way, they found it easy to ignore what went on and, even if they were not totally convinced, a reluctant loyalty can be seen. Thus, for most Germans their expressions of dissatisfaction were likely only to extend to complaining privately (Johnson), as they were aware of the terror that did exist if this was expressed publicly. Equally though, there was no safe available outlet where the dissatisfied could express even mild discontent. As Evans highlights, the removal of previous 'social and cultural surroundings', part of the process of *gleichschaltung*, was in part consciously planned by the Nazis to deny the opportunity for resistance. That 22 million Germans were members of the DAF by 1939 shows Johnson is correct to say 'most found little difficulty in conforming', at least outwardly, but there was little choice, as all independent trades unions had been closed in 1933, paving the way for this. It is likely that those who suffered most from this were working-class Germans, from which the bulk of support for the SPD and communists had been drawn. These parties had gained upwards of 30% of the votes before the ☞

The student has actually linked the views of Sources 1 and 3 to the points examined above. There is some analysis, although this is not fully explored. A better approach would be to integrate the discussion of the sources with own knowledge, using this to analyse the relative merits of their arguments and reach judgement over the significance of this issue.

Additionally, the answer could be improved by including more of the relevant material from the sources, as there are other parts of Sources 1 and 3 that relate to the issue under discussion, and Source 2 has been neglected altogether. While not all of the sources will be used for every point, a good answer will be structured clearly around arguments and will seek to make the very most of the sources.

The final main point is a relative strength of the essay. If the whole essay had been of this quality, it would have reached level 4. There is a clearer focus on the debate and the sources are used thoroughly, making several references to Johnson and also Evans. To improve further, the discussion between them could be addressed more directly.

Again, specific and relevant own knowledge is used to analyse the issue under discussion and also the views of the sources. To improve further, the student could reach a clear and reasoned judgement on the extent and influence of intimidation, focused on the question and linked clearly to the analysis within the paragraph. The student could also integrate the sources and own knowledge more tightly, by making more direct connections between the different sources (including cross-referencing their arguments over intimidation) and between the sources and own knowledge.

Nazis took power. As with the banning of the political parties, closing down trades unions was important in helping the Nazis control all Germans.

In conclusion, the sources do show that intimidation was used, but they also show how many Germans were happy with the regime and even supported the use of intimidation against certain groups, or at least tolerated this. Evans is right to highlight how 'fear and terror' were important 'political weapons from the very beginning'. However, once organised opposition was broken down, most Germans were not under direct threat and 'enjoyed their lives' as Johnson shows, so agreement was more due to improved economic conditions. While there was some intimidation, as most ordinary Germans wanted to avoid sanctions, they saw these as really being aimed at the enemies of Nazi Germany.

A conclusion is reached that offers and explains a judgement that is related to the views of two of the sources. The conclusion could be a little more directly focused and decisive in its judgement. However, the main issue for the conclusion is that it is only loosely related to main points. For level 4 and above, judgement needs to be more sustained.

Overall, this answer has the qualities of a level 3 response for both Assessment Objectives:

- It is able to analyse some key points of the arguments offered in the source material, clearly examining the different views they take on Nazi intimidation.
- It does reach a judgement on the importance of intimidation in gaining consent, which is supported by information from the sources and own knowledge.
- It does recognise the interpretations in the given extracts, setting Evans' emphasis on terror against the differing views of Johnson and Gellately, and offers some analysis of these, developing points of challenge and support for the view in the question.
- It uses accurate own knowledge, although this is not always clearly directed at the points under discussion and, at times, detail on the role of groups such as the *Gestapo* is not fully linked to the controversy in the sources.
- The argument shows some direction and control, although the focus is not sustained on the debate on the role intimidation played.

This answer would achieve **high level 3 and 10 marks for AO1a and b, high level 3 and 13 marks for AO2b, and overall would gain 23 marks**.

Grade A* student answer

Evans offers the strongest evidence that brutality and terror were the source of Nazi control, with the argument that 'the regime intimidated Germans into agreement' being from Source 1. While Sources 2 and 3 do accept that coercion existed in Nazi Germany, they place greater emphasis on other explanations for control, with Johnson emphasising most Germans not being intimidated, seeing the police state as being directed at internal enemies and this for their own protection. Gellately also argues this case, although suggesting a somewhat more active support for this among the masses, also emphasising the role media and word of mouth played in this. Thus it is clear that while the extent to which coercion and intimidation were used is open to discussion, there is no little doubt that it was significant. Therefore the greatest debate centres on the extent to which different sections of German society were, or indeed believed themselves to be, affected by this.

Source 1 suggests that intimidation 'loomed over everyone' through the threat of arrest and punishment. While Sources 2 and 3 accept the existence of such sanctions, highlighting 'a strong police presence' and camps 'in which the state confined "political criminals"', they place a very different emphasis on the nature of this and the extent to which ordinary Germans were intimidated by this. Johnson argues that most German's accepted the 'excess of laws' as they perceived them as being 'there to protect them'. Similarly, Gellately suggests that most Germans supported the 'new police' and perceived the camps as corrective 'boot-camps' for asocials. To an extent these views are valid; the level of popular support for these measures has resonance with the argument of Kershaw that there was a genuine existence of an emotional need for strong government and a tradition of authoritarian leadership. While the nature of the regime makes this hard to validate, the repeated popularity of the regime in the plebiscites of 1936 and 1938 suggest this to be so, and the estimated 25000 inmates of camps by 1939 pales against the millions of Germans who participated in Nazi organisations, suggesting Johnson is right to suggest Nazis' terror largely held no 'real threat to most ordinary Germans'. The intimidation clearly existed, but for many Germans this was directed at others and so did not 'loom' over them. ☞

This well-focused introduction sets out to offer a high-level response. The views of the different sources are clearly outlined, establishing the emphasis they place on different issues. The student offers a provisional judgement on this. This serves two purposes: setting out the direction of the main body of the essay, where the detailed analysis will take place, and giving the examiner a clear indication that this is an answer that can sustain analysis and evaluative argument. These are both level 5 skills.

In this first main paragraph, the student demonstrates an ability to cross-reference the arguments of all three sources. They examine in detail similarities and differences between the sources and also make subtle distinctions between them, such as between the views of Johnson and Gellately. Detailed own knowledge is used to examine the merits of these arguments, and a critical evaluation is then given that is explicitly focused on both the question and the point dealt with in this paragraph.

However, while there may have been the general 'popular support' that Gellately points to, it was not the *real threat* of an 'excess of laws' that intimidated ordinary Germans, but the all-encompassing authority of the police state. The Emergency Power Decree of February 1933 may have legitimated the expanding SS–police authority under Himmler's control, but it was the arbitrary ability to arrest Germans that caused fear, with 162 000 being placed in 'protective custody' without trial from 1933 to 1939. Thus Evans' argument that this intimidation was not 'levelled exclusively' against enemies of the state holds credibility; many Germans may have 'slept soundly', but they were only a denunciation – often for false or personal motives rather than political – away from arrest. In a sense, Gellately's point concerning the role media played in this goes some way to reconciling these views. The 'Gestapo, Kripo' and camps were distant from most as Gellately states, and even the SD, with 50 000 officers under Heydrich's command, were not oppressive to most Germans on a daily basis. However, all Germans were aware of what could and did happen to opponents, while the press, radio and 'word of mouth' were crucial for adding the element of uncertainty that meant that the fear, rather than the actual terror, within the 'fear and terror' that Evans sees as being integral, was the more significant in gaining the consent of ordinary Germans on a day-to-day basis.

That said, while it has to be accepted that intimidation played a significant role, it is harder to ascertain the degree of influence this had, and on what proportion of Germans. Johnson's assertion that most of those Germans who fitted the Nazi idea of the *volk* 'enjoyed their lives' under Nazi rule is convincing in this respect. While there were protests over food prices in 1935, and the high proportion of political prisoners in the likes of Dortmund prison who were listed as industrial workers shows higher levels of dissatisfaction among such a group, many were appeased by the increased employment Johnson highlights, and in this sense a reluctant loyalty can be seen. Thus, for most Germans their expressions of dissatisfaction were likely only to extend to complaining privately (Johnson), as on balance they were aware of the terror that did exist if this was expressed publicly, and to some degree accepted the trade-off of apparent economic and foreign policy successes. Equally though, part of this equation was the lack of available outlets where even the dissatisfied could express ☞

Here, an issue linking from the previous point is developed. The student presents a focused argument that draws on well-chosen own knowledge, and is closely integrated with the arguments and evidence from the sources. While here only two of the sources are used, the response consistently returns to their evidence while sustaining an analysis that is directly focused on the question. A clear judgement is given, which evaluates the issues raised from the given extracts.

Although this is excellent work, there are opportunities to develop it further. The student could have made more of the implications of Gellately's evidence, in how the impression of coercion was created in the minds of ordinary Germans. Additionally, the student could have brought in Source 2 here, using it to examine Johnson's point concerning how ordinary Germans believed that, in doing this, the state was protecting them. However it is not essential to use all three sources with every point made and, even at the highest level, you are not expected to cover every possible aspect. What is important is that key issues are dealt with, and your answer is organised effectively around them in order to allow you to maximise your exploration of the evidence on the controversy.

Again, this paragraph highlights a strong understanding of the views the sources take towards the debate, with a focused and critical argument being explored that links from previous points. The student again uses specific own knowledge and thoroughly explores the evidence of the sources.

They have made confident arguments concerning the relative strengths of the arguments the sources make. While you are not expected either to debunk or to disprove the views of professional historians, being confident in identifying and assessing the arguments offered is essential for the top level. This is achieved by both a confident understanding of the key issues and arguments in the controversy, with the knowledge to explore these, and a clear and careful reading of the extracts to identify the issues and arguments they focus on.

even mild discontent. As Evans highlights, the removal of previous 'social and cultural surroundings', part of the process of *gleichschaltung*, was in part consciously planned by the Nazis to deny the opportunity for resistance. That 22 million Germans were members of the DAF by 1939 shows Johnson is correct to say 'most found little difficulty in conforming', at least outwardly, but the violent seizure of the socialist ADGB union in May 1933 and the closure of other trades unions – some voluntarily, but under clear threat – paved the way for this. Therefore Evans is correct to see this as part of Nazi coercion 'from the very beginning'. While Gellately argues there was 'much popular support' for action against political opponents, this does not exclude the 30% or more who supported left-wing parties, the bulk of whom SOPADE reports suggest turned towards their private life, partly as a result of the intimidation highlighted above, which set the tone from early in the regime. Germans may not have been constantly faced by intimidation from the Nazis, but the threat was sufficient to dissuade the vast majority.

In conclusion, it is clear that coercion and intimidation were crucial tools for the Nazis in controlling the German population. While Gellately is correct to point to how most Germans did not have regular contact with the various arms of the police state, and it may indeed have had popular support for attacks on the workshy and others deemed asocial and against the nation, that did not mean the existence of such institutions played no role in conformity, as people realised the threat the police state posed and so hid any criticisms they had. The measures and methods that Evans argues over were crucial from the very beginning, as they created an environment in which people modified their activities and agreed with the state. This was partly a result of the benefits the Nazis brought; nevertheless, while most Germans were not in direct and immediate danger, the very existence of the *Gestapo*, camps and other arbitrary measures did create fear and so intimidated ordinary Germans into agreement.

The conclusion is directly focused on the question, offering a clear evaluation that draws together the different strands of argument. This flows directly from the arguments established in the introduction and examined throughout the essay, with clear reasoning and critical distinction over the nature and extent of the role intimidation played in gaining consent. Additionally, these are related to the views of the given extracts.

Overall, this answer has the qualities of a level 5 response for both Assessment Objectives.

This answer has a sustained and direct focus on the specific demands of the question, examining the role intimidation played in the light of the differing interpretations.

- There is confident analysis of the sources, weighing Evans' arguments over fear and terror against the two differing perspectives on consent offered by Gellately and Johnson.

- Own knowledge is used to examine the debate, being well selected and closely integrated with the evidence from the sources.

- Throughout the answer, reasoned judgements are offered on the nature and extent of coercion.

- While there are issues that could be developed even further, such as the difficulties in measuring genuine consent, the answer offers a convincing evaluation within the time constraints given.

This answer would achieve **level 5 and 16 marks for AO1a and b, level 5 and 24 marks for AO2b, and overall would gain the full 40 marks**.